THE MYSTERY OF EDWIN DROOD

THE MYSTERY OF EDWIN DROOD

A new musical
by
Rupert Holmes

suggested by
Charles Dickens' uncompleted novel

Nelson Doubleday, Inc.
GARDEN CITY, NEW YORK

The Mystery of Edwin Drood
is forever dedicated to the lovely memory of

WENDY ISOBEL HOLMES

(1976–1986)

Manufactured in the United States of America

ACKNOWLEDGEMENTS

Well before DROOD went into rehearsal, I learned that the play I had labored over during the course of two years was no longer exclusively mine, and that much of what I'd written had become, in effect, a kind of rule book for a rather intricate parlor game intended to occupy a few hours of an evening with friends.

I hope it's clear to all by now that what follows was never intended to be a serious Dickensian adaptation. Rather, it was always conceived as a springboard for a series of theatrical moments and events, using a literary curiosity as trampoline. And for all this lofty talk, my goal has always been one with the Music Hall Royale's: to amuse, divert, and entertain the patrons at almost any cost.

Wilford Leach, its director, has redefined that term by being my cohort and co-conspirator, my editor, my touchstone, and my dear friend. Likewise Graciela Daniele, its choreographer, has infused her vivacious and resolute humanity throughout these pages. DROOD's frighteningly over-talented cast found humor in lines that I took too seriously, and found laughter in jokes that had precious little humor in them. In particular, George Rose, who performed Act One of this DROOD before I had begun to write Act Two, bolstered the play with his consummate professionalism and masterful wit.

To Normand Kurtz, who sustained this dream through all my waking hours . . . to Deborah Grunfeld, whose insights and musicality sustained me and preserved this show through endless hours, weeks, and months . . . to Rob Main, who saw to it that the volume you hold could exist . . . to Gail Merrifield, who nurtured this sapling of an idea by a sappy author . . . and to Joseph Papp, without whose courage and genius "DROOD" would never have been seen or heard outside my living room . . . my irrevocable gratitude.

ACKNOWLEDGEMENTS

Lastly, to my parents, Gwen and Leonard, to my brother Richard, and to my darling wife, Liza Holmes, Attorney-at-Law . . . who lived DROOD through every moment of its existence . . .

And to my beloved daughter, Wendy Isobel Holmes, who left us unexpectedly in this our happiest year, and who lives and laughs between the lines and pages of this volume . . . my inadequate but eternal devotion.

Rupert Holmes
New York, 1986

The Mystery of Edwin Drood was originally presented by Joseph Papp as a New York Shakespeare Festival production at the Delacorte Theatre in Central Park, New York City on August 21, 1985 with the following cast (in order of appearance):

Your Chairman, Mr. William Cartwright/ *Mayor Thomas Sapsea*	GEORGE ROSE
John Jasper/*Mr. Clive Paget*	HOWARD MCGILLIN
The Reverend Mr. Crisparkle/ *Mr. Wilfred Barking-Smythe*	LARRY SHUE
Edwin Drood/*Miss Alice Nutting*	BETTY BUCKLEY
Rosa Bud/*Miss Deirdre Peregrine*	PATTI COHENOUR
Alice/*Miss Isabel Yearsley*	JUDY KUHN
Beatrice/*Miss Florence Gill*	DONNA MURPHY
Helena Landless/*Miss Janet Conover*	JANA SCHNEIDER
Neville Landless/*Mr. Victor Grinstead*	JOHN HERRERA
Durdles/*Mr. Nick Cricker*	JEROME DEMPSEY
Deputy/*Master Robert Bascomb*	DON KEHR
The Princess Puffer/*Miss Angela Prysock*	CLEO LAINE
A Lascar/*Mr. Harry Sayle*	NICHOLAS GUNN
A Thuggee/*Mr. Montague Pruitt*	BRAD MISKELL
Clients of the Princess Puffer/	
Mr. James Throttle	ROBERT GROSSMAN
Mr. Alan Eliot	HERNDON LACKEY
Succubae/*Miss Gwendolen Pynn*	FRANCINE LANDES
Miss Sarah Cook	KAREN GIOMBETTI
Miss Florence Gill	DONNA MURPHY
Miss Isabel Yearsley	JUDY KUHN
Statue/*Mr. Christopher Lyon*	STEPHEN GLAVIN
Portrait/*Mr. Brian Pankhurst*	CHARLES GOFF
Harold/*Mr. James Throttle*	ROBERT GROSSMAN
Julian/*Mr. Alan Eliot*	HERNDON LACKEY
Horace/*Mr. Brian Pankhurst*	CHARLES GOFF
Bazzard/*Mr. Phillip Bax*	JOE GRIFASI
Dick Datchery	???????
Citizens of Cloisterham	KAREN GIOMBETTI, STEPHEN GLAVIN, CHARLES GOFF, NICHOLAS GUNN, ROBERT GROSSMAN, JUDY KUHN, HERNDON LACKEY, FRANCINE LANDES, BRAD MISKELL, DONNA MURPHY

The production, with some minor changes, re-opened at the Imperial Theatre, New York City on December 2, 1985 with the following cast:

Mayor Thomas Sapsea/*Mr. William Cartwright, Your Chairman*	GEORGE ROSE
Stage Manager and Barkeep/*Mr. James Throttle*	PETER MCROBBIE
John Jasper/*Mr. Clive Paget*	HOWARD MCGILLIN
The Reverend Mr. Crisparkle/*Mr. Cedric Moncrieffe*	GEORGE N. MARTIN
Edwin Drood/*Miss Alice Nutting*	BETTY BUCKLEY
Rosa Bud/*Miss Deirdre Peregrine*	PATTI COHENOUR
Alice/*Miss Isabel Yearsley*	JUDY KUHN
Beatrice/*Miss Florence Gill*	DONNA MURPHY
Helena Landless/*Miss Janet Conover*	JANA SCHNEIDER
Neville Landless/*Mr. Victor Grinstead*	JOHN HERRERA
Durdles/*Mr. Nick Cricker*	JEROME DEMPSEY
Deputy/*Master Nick Cricker*	STEPHEN GLAVIN
The Princess Puffer/*Miss Angela Prysock*	CLEO LAINE
Shade of Jasper/*Mr. Harry Sayle*	NICHOLAS GUNN
Shade of Drood/*Mr. Montague Pruitt*	BRAD MISKELL
Clients of the Princess Puffer/	
Mr. Alan Eliot	HERNDON LACKEY
Mr. Christopher Lyon	ROB MARSHALL
Succubae/*Miss Gwendolen Pynn*	FRANCINE LANDES
Miss Sarah Cook	KAREN GIOMBETTI
Miss Florence Gill	DONNA MURPHY
Miss Isabel Yearsley	JUDY KUHN
Statue/*Master Nick Cricker*	STEPHEN GLAVIN
Servants/*Mr. Philip Bax*	JOE GRIFASI
Miss Violet Balfour	SUSAN GOODMAN
Miss Gwendolen Pynn	FRANCINE LANDES
Harold/*Mr. James Throttle*	PETER MCROBBIE
Julian/*Mr. Alan Eliot*	HERNDON LACKEY
Horace/*Mr. Brian Pankhurst*	CHARLES GOFF
Bazzard/*Mr. Phillip Bax*	JOE GRIFASI
Dick Datchery	???????

Citizens of Cloisterham	KAREN GIOMBETTI, CHARLES GOFF, SUSAN GOODMAN, NICHOLAS GUNN, JUDY KUHN, HERNDON LACKEY, FRANCINE LANDES, ROB MARSHALL, PETER MCROBBIE, BRAD MISKELL, DONNA MURPHY

Directed by	WILFORD LEACH
Choreography by	GRACIELA DANIELE
Scenery by	BOB SHAW
Costumes by	LINDSAY W. DAVIS
Lighting by	PAUL GALLO
Sound Design by	TOM MORSE
Magic Lantern Projections by	JAMES COCHRANE
Hair & Wigs by	PAUL HUNTLEY
Musical Direction by	MICHAEL STAROBIN
Orchestrations by	RUPERT HOLMES
Associate Producer	JASON STEVEN COHEN

CAST OF CHARACTERS

(in order of appearance)

Mr. Thomas Purcell, maestro of the Music Hall Royale Orchestra

Mr. William Cartwright, Chairman

JOHN JASPER	Mr. Clive Paget
THE REVEREND MR. CRISPARKLE	Mr. Cedric Moncrieffe
EDWIN DROOD	Miss Alice Nutting
ROSA BUD	Miss Deirdre Peregrine
ALICE	Miss Isabel Yearsley
BEATRICE	Miss Florence Gill
HELENA LANDLESS	Miss Janet Conover
NEVILLE LANDLESS	Mr. Victor Grinstead
MAYOR THOMAS SAPSEA	Mr. James Hitchens
DURDLES	Mr. Nick Cricker
DEPUTY	Master Nick Cricker
THE PRINCESS PUFFER	Miss Angela Prysock
SHADE OF DROOD	Mr. Harry Sayle
SHADE OF JASPER	Mr. Montague Pruitt
CLIENTS OF PRINCESS PUFFER	Mr. Alan Eliot
	Mr. Christopher Lyon
SUCCUBAE	Miss Gwendolen Pynn, Miss Sarah Cook
	Miss Florence Gill, Miss Isabel Yearsley
SATYR	Master Nick Cricker
HORACE	Mr. Brian Pankhurst
BAZZARD	Mr. Phillip Bax
DICK DATCHERY	???????

CITIZENS OF CLOISTERHAM	Mr. Philip Bax, Miss Sarah Cook
	Mr. Alan Eliot, Miss Florence Gill
	Mr. Christopher Lyon, Mr. Medford Moss
	Mr. Brian Pankhurst, Mr. Montague Pruitt
	Miss Gwendolen Pynn, Mr. Harry Sayle
	Mr. James Throttle, Miss Isabel Yearsley

STAGE MANAGER AND BARKEEP	Mr. James Throttle

The time is the present, 1873.

THE MUSIC HALL ROYALE

programme for this evening:
Opening comments by Your Chairman, Mr. William Cartwright,
immediately followed by:
The Music Hall Royale's Presentation of

THE MYSTERY OF EDWIN DROOD

MUSICAL NUMBERS

ACT I: THE SITUATION

"There You Are" . . . . Chairman & Company

Scene I

The home of John Jasper at Minor Canon Corner in the cathedral city of Cloisterham. A morning in late December.

"A Man Could Go Quite Mad" . . . . Jasper
"Two Kinsmen" . . . . Drood & Jasper

Scene II

The conservatory at the Nun's House, a seminary for young women in Cloisterham High Street. Later that morning.

"Moonfall" . . . . Rosa
"Moonfall" (reprise) . . . . Rosa & Helena, with Alice & Beatrice

Scene III

Cloisterham High Street, outside the residence of Mayor Thomas Sapsea. The following afternoon.

Scene IV

The opium den of Princess Puffer in the East End of London. Dawn, the next day.

"The Wages of Sin" . . . . Puffer
"Jasper's Vision" . . . . . . Shades of Jasper & Drood; Succubae & Satyr

(continued)

Scene V
Cloisterham High Street. That afternoon.
"Ceylon" . . . . Drood, Rosa, Helena & Neville, with ensemble
"Both Sides of the Coin" . . . . Jasper & Chairman, with ensemble

Scene VI
The crypts of Cloisterham Cathedral. Late that night.

Scene VII
The ruins of Cloisterham. Christmas eve.
"Perfect Strangers" . . . . Drood & Rosa

Scene VIII
The home of John Jasper. A short time later.
"No Good Can Come From Bad" . . . . Neville, Drood, Rosa, Helena, Crisparkle, Jasper & Bazzard

Scene IX
Minor Canon Corner. Christmas day and night.
"Never the Luck" . . . . Bazzard
"The Name of Love" & "Moonfall" (reprise) . . . . Rosa & Jasper, with ensemble

THE MYSTERY OF EDWIN DROOD
is performed with one fifteen-minute interval

ACT II: THE SLEUTHS

Scene I
Cloisterham Station. Six months later.
"Settling Up the Score" . . . . Datchery & Puffer, with ensemble

Scene II
Cloisterham High Street.
"Off to the Races" . . . . . Chairman, Durdles & Deputy, with ensemble
"Don't Quit While You're Ahead" . . . . Puffer & Company

THE VOTING
"Settling Up the Score" (reprise) . . . . Company
immediately followed by
"The Garden Path to Hell" . . . . Puffer

(continued)

and

THE SOLUTION

"Puffer's Confession . . . . Puffer
"Out on a Limerick" . . . . Datchery, with Company
"Jasper's Confession" . . . . Jasper
"Murderer's Confession" . . . . ?????
"Perfect Strangers" (reprise) . . . . The Lovers, with Company
"The Writing on the Wall" . . . . Drood, with Company
"Don't Quit While You're Ahead" (reprise) . . . . Chairman & Company

PRELUDE

The time is the present: 1873. The audience finds that it has entered the permanent lodgings of London's own Music Hall Royale, (Mr. William Cartwright, chairman). The theatre seems dressed for the occasion, and regulars of "the Roy" sense that something beyond their favourite performers' usual farrago of music hall songs and comedy turns, (performed to the constant accompaniment of best ale, bubbly wine, and spirits), may be in the offing. One notable clue is the curtain itself, newly-acquired from a light opera company in Newcastle, upon which has been embroidered curious scenes of crypts and cathedrals, along with the ornately-lettered words: THE MYSTERY OF EDWIN DROOD.

Just as we have made some progress with our playbill, (and even more successfully progressed through our second glass of hock), we are distracted by a rather beery voice next to us in the aisle. It's Nick Cricker himself. Odd that he would venture out into the audience before the show. He greets us with a few jests that have long lain in the public domain and is now saying something about our determining the outcome of the evening's programme. Man must be drunk. "Voting", he's going on about.

And as we try to decipher his words, another voice commences to hawk salutations like a monger of jellied eels. It's Moncrieffe. Thought the man had more dignity than that. He's addressing another section of the audience, apparently about the same matter that Cricker's going on about. Suddenly, a loud cry of "Drooood" emanates from the residents of the cheaper seats. Sounds like Grinstead, the new fellow, leading the "huzzahs". Trust him to curry favour with the audience before the overture.

The theatre has become quite clamorous indeed, and most of us are too busy craning our necks to actually listen. The aisles are full with company members—all the way up to the two-penny seats. Nice bit of ankle on Deirdre there. Has madness taken over?

Beneath this din, the Royale orchestra, each member of which owns his own instrument, sounds a heraldic call—and now pandemonium truly reigns. The actors are everywhere to be heard, and as many of them are not yet fully in costume, everywhere to be seen as well. My god, I saw less of my wife on our honeymoon than I'm seeing of that fetching thing there. Ought to be a law, but I won't enforce it.

The conductor, Mr. Thomas Purcell, cues the percussion battery into a brisk tempo, and here is William Cartwright himself, bursting through what few dancers have consented to remain on stage. We'll be all right now. Leave Cartwright to restore order.

ACT ONE

"THERE YOU ARE" (Chairman and Company)

CHAIRMAN:
WHAT'S A KING WITHOUT HIS CROWN?
TAKE AWAY HIS THRONE AND GOWN,
HE COULD BE THE RABBLE OR THE RUSSIAN CZAR
JUDGE EACH CREATURE OF OUR RACE
BY EACH FEATURE IN HIS FACE.
LOOK AT HIM—(I REST MY CASE), WELL THERE YOU ARE!
AND IT MATTERS NOT TO ME WHAT PART OF TOWN YOU'VE COME FROM;
WE BUT CHEER YOU'VE MADE IT HERE AT ALL!
HERE WITHIN THIS GARISH PARISH CALLED THE MUSIC HALL . . .

CHAIRMAN AND COMPANY:
AND THERE YOU ARE!

CHAIRMAN:
HOW VERY GLAD WE ARE

CHAIRMAN AND COMPANY:
THAT THERE YOU ARE!

CHAIRMAN:
IT ISN'T WHO YOU ARE BUT

CHAIRMAN AND COMPANY:
WHERE YOU ARE,
AND THERE YOU ARE,
AND GRATEFUL ARE WE TO SEE

CHAIRMAN:
HOW FINE AND

CHAIRMAN AND COMPANY:
FAIR YOU ARE!
THERE YOU ARE!

CHAIRMAN: *(Calling out into audience)* Angela! Angela, my dear, are you out there?

PRYSOCK: *(From amid people in box seats)* I'm up here in the Royal Box, Bill!

CHAIRMAN: Ah, there you are! And who's that you're with then?

PRYSOCK:
I AM STANDING WITH A GENT
WHO SEEMS SINGULARLY BENT
ON ATTACHING BOTH HIS HANDS TO BOTH MY KNEES!

CHAIRMAN: Alice!

NUTTING: *(From balcony)*
I'M CONSIDERING THE LAP
OF A MOST ENGAGING CHAP
AND I'LL LET HIM DO EXACTLY AS *I* PLEASE!

CHAIRMAN: Clive!

PAGET:
I'VE A LADY DOWN IN FRONT WHO'S HANDED ME HER LATCH KEY—
SURELY SHE MUST KNOW THAT SPELLS HER DOOM!

CHAIRMAN: Deirdre!

PEREGRINE:
AND THIS MAN HAS GRAND DESIGNS TO SHOW ME
IN MY DRESSING ROOM . . .

CHAIRMAN AND COMPANY:
OH, THERE YOU ARE!
HOW DISTINGUÉ AND DEBONAIR YOU ARE . . .
JUST SLIGHTLY WEST OF LEICESTER SQUARE YOU ARE
YES, THERE YOU ARE!
THAT THANKFUL WE ALL SHOULD BE FULL WELL-AWARE
WE ARE.
SO LIGHTNING QUICK LET'S ALL KICK UP A FUSS!

WE CAN BUT PRAY YOUR TRUST IS
BLIND IN US.
SO DRINK YOUR FILL AND JUST UNWIND IN US!
A WARMLY WICKED FRAME OF MIND IN US
YOU'LL FIND IN US.
WE WANT YOU! AND NOT A LOT WE CARE FOR WHERE
YOU'VE BEEN,
AND NOT A JOT WE CARE HOW YOU'VE GOT IN:
WE BUT CARE THAT THERE YOU ARE!

Damned if there you are!

(The Chairman, Mr. William Cartwright, goes immediately into his introductory remarks. He is instantly and indisputably in charge of both the situation and the evening)

CHAIRMAN: Thank you, thank you so very much. Good evening and welcome, a very warm welcome indeed to all of you on this most thrilling of evenings to the Music Hall Royale. Ladies and gentlemen, this evening we have the honour and privilege of presenting for your approval: the premiere performance of . . . *(He reaches for his gavel)* The Mystery . . . *(Two sharp raps of same)*

CHAIRMAN AND COMPANY: Of Edwin Drood!

(A final rap)

CHAIRMAN: This being a Musicale with Dramatic Interludes. Now, as you are no doubt aware, our own Mr. Charles Dickens was full halfway through the creation of The Greatest Mystery Novel of Our Time, when he committed the one ungenerous deed of his noble career: He Died, leaving behind not the slightest hint as to the outcome he intended for his bizarre and uncompleted puzzle: The Mystery Of Edwin Drood. Tonight, however, ladies and gentlemen, when together we reach that point in our story beyond which Charles Dickens wrote No More, I shall be asking you to Vote upon key questions regarding the outcome of our plot. Our company will then make its most earnest effort to meet this supreme challenge: to contrive An Ending in Accordance with Your Specifications. *(Purcell cuts off orchestra)* So come on, let's all be vulgar and uncivilized as is legally possible! *(Moving towards edge of stage)* Kick off your shoes, let out your belts and corsets . . . and enjoy yourselves. By the way, for those among you who arrived alone and require companionship up through the final curtain . . .

COMPANY: Or Beyond . . . *(Massive implications here)*

CHAIRMAN: You need only speak to our stage manager, Mr. James Throttle, whose pleasure it is to see

THROTTLE: That you need never be lonely again.

CHAIRMAN: But, please remember, these sparkling and vivacious ingenues are not salaried employees, and so we do ask you to contribute generously towards the cost of their Theatrical Studies . . . and that you make sure all goods are returned tomorrow morning . . .

COMPANY: None the Worse for Wear.

CHAIRMAN: So by all means let us proceed with this evening's bill of fare: for the first time ever, the completed musical rendition of . . . *(Gavel once)* The Mystery . . . *(Gavel twice)*

CHAIRMAN AND COMPANY: Of Edwin Drood! !

(Gothic fanfare)

CHAIRMAN: Cloisterham! The ancient, mouldering cathedral city of Cloisterham! *(A church organ plays a sombre recessional hymn)* Not a particularly encouraging setting for the Christmas season now upon us. A wintry shudder goes through the giant elms as they shed a gust of tears. *(The curtains part to reveal the home of John Jasper, within which rests a portrait of Rosa Bud)* And here we are in the home of Mr. John Jasper, choirmaster of Cloisterham Cathedral. *(Enter Jasper in scarf, robe, and cassock, which, lost in thought, he removes)* Choirmaster, composer, organist, and vocal instructor, John Jasper is blessed with a voice the angels themselves might envy.

(Ecclesiastical music stops abruptly)

CHAIRMAN: *(Continues boldly)* And who, dear ladies and gentlemen, more suited to essay the role of John Jasper than that gifted vocalist himself, your very own MR. CLIVE PAGET!

(Brassy fanfare and huzzahs from the shills. Paget/Jasper is obviously the principal male of the Theatre Royale. With total disregard for the character he is portraying, Paget acknowledges the ensuing applause with a rakish smile, displaying several sets

of teeth. As the orchestra strikes a resounding chord, Paget instantly steps back into character)

"A MAN COULD GO QUITE MAD" (Jasper)

JASPER:
ANOTHER TRIFLING DAY,
ONE MORE SOUL-STIFLING DAY
OF BLINDING PAIN:
BOREDOM GRINDS MY BRAIN
DOWN TO THE GRAIN.

A MAN COULD GO QUITE MAD
AND NOT BE ALL THAT BAD.
CONSIDER EACH SUPERB, DISTURBING URGE YOU'VE EVER HAD,
TO CURSE ALOUD IN CHURCH
OR CHOKE EACH BLOKE WHO THROWS A SMILE YOUR WAY . . .
BE THAT AS IT MAY,

A MAN COULD HAVE BAD DREAMS
AND NOT BE ALL HE SEEMS,
YET NOT BE FAR-REMOVED FROM ALL THE NOBLEST OF EXTREMES.
SOMETIMES I THINK THAT SANITY IS JUST A PASSING FAD.
A MAN COULD GO QUITE MAD!

UNBLESSED ARE THE DULL.
ONE CEASELESS, PEACELESS LULL.
SOME WOND'ROUS NIGHT,
STORM-STRUCK THUND'ROUS LIGHT
WILL CAST ME RIGHT.

A SCULPTOR LACKING ARMS,
A SORC'ROR LACKING CHARMS,

A FIEND WHO FRIGHTENS NO ONE FOR THERE'S NO ONE THAT HE HARMS,
WHOSE CLUTCHES CLUTCH AT ONLY DESP'RATE RESPITE
FROM THIS DIM TABLEAU!
KNOWING THIS IS SO,
I HIDE MYSELF IN THOUGHT,
WHERE ONE CANNOT BE CAUGHT,
AND FEED ON DREAMS THAT CONTRADICT EACH EDICT I'VE BEEN TAUGHT.
AND IF SOMEDAY I LOSE MY WAY AND MIND, YOU'LL FIND ME GLAD—
A MAN COULD GO QUITE, MAN COULD GO QUITE,
MAN COULD GO QUITE MAD!

(The number concludes with a flourish. Paget/Jasper expects and accepts the applause, over which Chairman proclaims:)

CHAIRMAN: Your own Mr. Clive Paget, ladies and gentlemen! *(As applause dies down, Chairman admonishes the audience)* I sincerely hope the moderation of your applause merely means you're conserving your energy towards the final curtain. But to continue: John Jasper's thoughts are distracted by the arrival of the Reverend Mr. Septimus Crisparkle, portrayed this evening by that favourite fixture of the Music Hall Royale, Mr. Cedric Moncrieffe.

(Amiable fanfare. Enter Crisparkle)

CRISPARKLE: Sorry to hear you have not been well, Jasper! You do look a little worn.

JASPER: Do I? Oh, I don't think so. What is better, I don't feel so.

CRISPARKLE: I'm glad to hear that you expect young Drood.

JASPER: I expect the dear fellow every moment.

CRISPARKLE: Ah, he will do you more good than a doctor, Jasper.

JASPER: *(Sincerely)* More good than a dozen doctors. For I love him dearly, and I don't like doctors, or doctors' stuff!

DROOD: *(Off)* Hallo, uncle!

CRISPARKLE: Why, there's the lad now! I'll leave you to him!

(Crisparkle exits, perhaps waving in the direction of the approaching Drood, who appears, framed in the doorway)

DROOD: My dear uncle!

(They embrace. Tableau)

CHAIRMAN: *(Rising from his desk)* Ladies and gentlemen, Miss Alice Nutting! *(Fanfare as Chairman leads applause. Drood/Nutting breaks her embrace with Jasper, bows winsomely. She wears moustache, cap, trousers, to charming effect. We are smitten)* Devotees of male impersonation are more used to seeing Miss Nutting in top hat and tails, when she does her inimitable rendition of "Aren't I Half a Toff?" But this evening, she hides her distinctive form beneath the garb of young Edwin Drood.

DROOD: Any dinner, Uncle?

JASPER: *(Pouring glasses of sherry)* You forget, Ned, that "Uncle" and "Nephew" are words prohibited here by express agreement.

DROOD: *(Accepting sherry from Jasper)* Of course you're right, John. After all, we do have only a half-dozen years or so between our ages. *(Jasper starts to sip his own port)* Halloa, Jack! Don't drink yet! I must propose a toast.

JASPER: A toast to what, Ned?

DROOD: To Rosa.

JASPER: *(Faintly)* Rosa.

DROOD: To the fair Miss Rosa Bud. Surely you've not forgotten that Rosa and I are soon to be wed?

JASPER: It has not quite slipped my mind.

DROOD: Yes, a tedious ceremony in your creaking Cathedral, John, then off with my wonderfully pretty child-bride to dusty Egypt, where I intend to shake things up a bit!

JASPER: It is certain, then? Egypt seems a desperate great distance.

DROOD: Indeed it is, John. *(Studying painting)* You know, this portrait of Rosa is not one of my better efforts. Yet, you choose to hang it here. In heaven's name, Why?

JASPER: Because it reminds me of you, Ned. And of the happiness I wish you and Rosa.

DROOD: *(Moodily)* Oh, I'm sure we'll be quite happy . . . though our courtship suffers from an unavoidable flatness, owing to the fact that *my* dead and gone father and *her* dead and gone father had as good as married us at birth. Why the devil couldn't they have left us alone?

JASPER: Tut, tut, dear boy—

DROOD: Tut, tut? Yes, Jack, it's all very well for *you.* You have the freedom to love whomsoever you choose. *(He stops himself, alarmed by something he sees in Jasper's face)*

JASPER: Don't stop, dear fellow, do go on.

DROOD: Have I hurt your feelings, John?

JASPER: How could you have hurt my feelings? *(He immediately staggers back against whatever furniture will support him)*

DROOD: Good heavens, Jack, you look frightfully ill! There's a strange film come over your eyes!

JASPER: *(Forcing a smile and straightening himself)* I—I have been taking—medicine for a pain—an agony that overcomes me. I've been forced of late to seek—treatment in London for my condition. Fear not, the effects will soon be gone.

DROOD: My dear uncle!

JASPER: Then take it as a warning! And Ned . . . Edwin . . . this is a confidence between us.

DROOD: It shall be sacredly preserved, John.

JASPER: I have confided in you because—

DROOD: Because we are fast friends, and because you love and trust me as I love and trust you! Both hands, Jack!

(They clasp crossed hands)

"TWO KINSMEN" (Drood and Jasper)

DROOD:
MY DEAREST UNCLE JACK!

JASPER:
MY DEAREST NEPHEW NED!

BOTH:
A LIFE WITHOUT YOUR FRIENDSHIP
WOULD BE LIFE AS GOOD AS DEAD!

JASPER:
THE WINDS OF HELL MAY BLOW,
BUT AS YOU WELL MAY KNOW,
I'LL HEED YOUR CALL,
NO NEED TOO SMALL,
AND FACE THE FIRE BELOW
FOR YOU!

DROOD:
FOR YOU!

JASPER:
FOR YOU!

DROOD:
FOR YOU!

BOTH:
TWO KINSMEN, MORE THAN BROTHERS!
WE KNOW NO NEXT OF KIN
AND YET WE KNOW NO OTHERS
CLOSER 'NEATH THE SKIN.
THE BLOOD THAT FLOWS BETWEEN US,

THE BONDS THAT TIE US TWAIN;
TWO KINSMEN, WHEN ALL OTHERS FLEE
THEN WE REMAIN!

JASPER:
MY DEAREST NEPHEW NED!

DROOD:
MY DEAREST UNCLE JACK!
IF MEN SAY WORDS AGAINST YOU,
I WOULD MAKE THEM TAKE THEM BACK!
A LOYAL LAD AM I
WHO'D BE BUT GLAD TO DIE,
IF BY MY DEATH
ONE EXTRA BREATH
OF LIFE FOR YOU I'D BUY.
'TIS TRUE!

JASPER:
'TIS TRUE!

DROOD:
FOR YOU!

JASPER:
FOR YOU!

BOTH:
TWO KINSMEN, MORE THAN BROTHERS!
WE KNOW NO NEXT OF KIN
AND YET WE KNOW NO OTHERS
CLOSER 'NEATH THE SKIN.
THE BLOOD THAT FLOWS BETWEEN US,
THE BONDS THAT TIE US TWAIN;

TWO KINSMEN, WHEN ALL OTHERS FLEE
THEN WE REMAIN!

DROOD:
'TIS TRUE!

JASPER:
'TIS TRUE!

DROOD:
FOR YOU!

JASPER:
FOR YOU!

BOTH:
TRUE KINSMEN ARE WE TWO!

CHAIRMAN: Miss Alice Nutting and Mr. Clive Paget, ladies and gentlemen! *(The two acknowledge audience and Chairman's applause, then exit together. As they do so:)* Thank you indeed for that splendid duo! At a shilling a seat, two voices at the same time seems almost an embarrassment of riches. Though looking at some of you down here, I doubt if you'd be embarrassed by much! But to continue our story: young Edwin Drood is visiting Cloisterham to offer his regards to his bride-to-be, the fair Miss Rosa Bud, who, like Drood, is an orphan. Rosa resides at Cloisterham's most respectable seminary for young ladies, aptly if not correctly named "The Nun's House." *(Revealed is the conservatory of The Nun's House, a charming room with a piano to one side near French windows, beyond which are trellises and the hint of foliage. Several young girls giggle and twitter about the room)* Ladies and gentlemen, in the part of Miss Rosa Bud this evening, that most delicate of English roses, that blossoming bud that has even yet to be plucked, the unspeakably lovely Miss Deirdre Peregrine!

(Peregrine/Rosa rushes "out" of the set and towards us. She curtsies and returns to the other girls. Jasper enters briskly, music manuscript in hand)

JASPER: Rosa, the happiest of birthdays to you! I only pray I may be able to say these words on each of your birthdays.

ROSA: I fear—I fear that is not likely, since, as you know, your own nephew Edwin and I will be departing for Egypt once we are married.

(Rosa's classmates run from room, giggling)

JASPER: It was only a wish, Rosa. How lovely you look! I have awaited your birthday with eagerness.

ROSA: Eagerness, Mr. Jasper?

JASPER: Yes, your voice will no longer be as subject to the fluctuations of adolescence. And in what condition is your voice today, my dearest student?

ROSA: As my tutor, perhaps that question should best be answered by you, Mr. Jasper. Shall I sing the Mozart?

JASPER: No. *(Handing her a manuscript)* I have composed a song especially for you, my loveliest subject, on the occasion of your birthday. A choirmaster's pay being what it is, my life's blood is the most I can afford to offer.

ROSA: Sir, I— *(She reads the music)* Mr. Jasper, I cannot sing these words. It would not be proper.

JASPER: Why, whatever can you mean?

ROSA: I do not—I am not worthy of it.

JASPER: As your music master, that should be my decision. From the beginning, please.

(She commences and there is tremendous tension, almost fear in her voice, as she watches Jasper watching her)

"MOONFALL" (Rosa)

ROSA:
BETWEEN THE VERY DEAD OF NIGHT AND DAY,
UPON A STEELY SHEET OF LIGHT, I'LL LAY,
AND IN THE MOONFALL, I'LL GIVE MYSELF TO YOU.
I'LL BATHE IN MOONFALL AND DRESS MYSELF IN DEW.

BEFORE THE CLOAK OF NIGHT REVEALS THE MORN,
TIME HOLDS ITS BREATH WHILE IT CONCEALS THE DAWN,
AND IN THE MOONFALL, ALL SOUND IS FROZEN STILL,
YET WARM AGAINST ME, YOUR SKIN WILL WARM THE CHILL OF

MOONFALL.
I FEEL ITS FINGERS.
LINGERS THE VEIL OF NIGHTSHADE,
LIGHT MADE FROM STARS THAT ALL-TOO-SOON FALL,
MOONFALL THAT POURS FROM YOU.

BETWIXT OUR HEARTS, LET NOTHING INTERVENE.
BETWEEN OUR EYES, THE ONLY SIGHT I'VE SEEN
IS LUST'ROUS MOONFALL AS IT BLINDS MY VIEW . . .
SO THAT SOON I ONLY SEE BUT YOU.

(Rosa returns to the piano, where she is near-hysterical from her emotional ordeal)

JASPER: That was lovely, Rosa.

ROSA: Thank you, sir.

JASPER: But "lovely" will not do. When you sing the words, you must make me feel you mean them! Once again, if you please.

(As he plays the introduction again, Helena and Neville Landless and Crisparkle enter and listen with interest as Rosa struggles to sing)

ROSA: "BETWEEN THE VERY DEAD OF NIGHT AND DAY . . . UPON A STEELY SHEET . . ." I can't bear this! I'm frightened! Take me away! !

(She collapses. Helena impulsively reaches for her and holds her consolingly. Neville, a deeply tanned young man, keeps his distance but is obviously fascinated by Rosa and puzzled by Jasper, who is virtually frozen at the piano. Helena eases Rosa into a chair, advising the others in an unplaceable Eastern accent ripe with curry and chutney:)

HELENA: It's nothing. It's all over. Don't speak to her for a minute and she'll be well.

CRISPARKLE: She's not used to an audience. Besides, Mr. Jasper, you are such a conscientious master that I believe you make her afraid of you. No wonder.

HELENA: No wonder.

CRISPARKLE: *(Trying to make a joke)* You'd be afraid of him under similar circumstances, wouldn't you, Miss Landless?

(Gong)

HELENA: *(Significantly)* Not under *any* circumstances.

(Sitar sting)

CHAIRMAN: *(Aside to audience)* Ladies and gentlemen, our own fiery spirit, the unpredictable Miss Janet Conover!

(Taj Mahal fanfare. She moves center, bows to audience splendidly and returns to her original place. Jasper rises from his frozen state)

CRISPARKLE: Mr. Jasper, let me introduce young Neville Landless. He and his twin sister, Helena, have both arrived from Ceylon, where they no longer have any family. Neville has been entrusted to my care, and Helena will be living here at the Nun's House.

JASPER: *(Adopting his most amenable face)* Welcome to Cloisterham, Mr. Landless.

CRISPARKLE: I'm afraid young Master Neville has been given over to me to calm his rather hot-tempered nature . . . and to help him make a new beginning here in Cloisterham.

JASPER: You and your sister lost your parents recently, Mr. Landless?

CRISPARKLE: *(Answering for Neville)* Their mother died in Ceylon when they were quite young. Now their stepfather has crossed over as well.

JASPER: I'm most sorry.

NEVILLE: There is no need for you bright gentlemen to console me. As it happens, it was well my stepfather died when he did, or I might have killed him.

(Ominous chord. Even the Chairman is startled by this comment, adding:)

CHAIRMAN: The newest member of our company, ladies and gentlemen, Mr. Victor Grinstead!

(Grinstead bows, eyeing the audience with suspicion as the orchestra repeats its musical sting)

NEVILLE: *(To Crisparkle)* I surprise you, sir?

CRISPARKLE: You shock me, unspeakably shock me.

NEVILLE: You never saw him beat my sister. My stepfather was a brute, Mr. Jasper. In desperation, Helena tried on more than one occasion to flee his cruel and miserly hand, even disguising herself as a boy. But to no avail. And as for myself, I have had, from my earliest remembrances, to subdue a deadly and bitter hatred, which has made me secret and revengeful.

(Secret and revengeful sting)

CRISPARKLE: I say . . .

NEVILLE: *(To Crisparkle)* However, sir, your kindness and goodwill has deeply moved me. I pledge to change my ill-tempered ways, and break new ground for myself.

CRISPARKLE: There's the lad! He'll soon blend in, Mr. Jasper.

NEVILLE: Your pupil, Mr. Jasper: she sings beautifully. Your labours have not been without success.

JASPER: I trust so, Mr. Landless.

NEVILLE: And may I enquire if your relationship extends beyond that of pupil and master—

CRISPARKLE: Heavens, no, Neville! Miss Bud is betrothed to young Edwin Drood, Mr. Jasper's nephew.

JASPER: You'd do well to cast your eyes and interests in other directions, sir.

NEVILLE: I beg your pardon, Mr. Jasper.

JASPER: *(Regarding Neville with caution)* No pardon is necessary. However, I must be off. Choir practice, I fear. I wish you well in your new life, Mr. Landless.

NEVILLE: Thank you, thank you indeed, Mr. Jasper. *(Meaningfully)* I trust we shall meet again. *(Indicative trilling from the orchestra as he watches Jasper exit Right; then, turning to Crisparkle:)* And I should like to meet this . . . Drood . . . and see what sort of man is worthy of the affection of Miss Bud.

CRISPARKLE: Steady, lad. Steady.

(As they exit, Crisparkle looks back with suspicion . . . or perhaps suspiciously. Orchestra quietly reprises "MOONFALL")

HELENA: You are feeling better now, aren't you?

ROSA: Oh much, thank you.

HELENA: These surroundings, which may seem very secure to you, are new and unsettling to me. You will be my friend, won't you?

ROSA: I will be as good a friend as such a mite of a thing can be to such a womanly and handsome creature as you.

(They kiss in sisterly fashion)

HELENA: Who is Mr. Jasper?

ROSA: *(Turning away)* My Edwin's uncle, and my music . . . master.

HELENA: You know that he loves you?

ROSA: *(Fearfully)* Oh don't! Don't! He terrifies me. I feel I am never safe from him. He has made a slave of me with his looks . . . forced me to keep silent without his uttering a single threat.

"MOONFALL"—reprise (Rosa, Helena, Wendy, Beatrice)

HELENA:	ROSA, WENDY, BEATRICE:
EACH ONE OF US WILL SOMETIME	
FEEL THE SAME	EACH ONE OF US MUST SOMETIME
WAY: TO MEET WITH LOVE, WE	WAIT TO MEET WITH LOVE AND NEVER
GO . . .	KNOW HIS NAME, HIS NAME,

ALL:

BUT IN THE MOONFALL SOON ALL FEARS ARE FEW,
SO THAT SOON I ONLY SEE BUT YOU.
SO THAT SOON I ONLY SEE BUT YOU.

CHAIRMAN: We now step from out the doorway of the Nun's House and fall in step with a relic known only to the residents of Cloisterham as "Durdles," a gentleman whose knowledge of the Cathedral tombs is exceeded only by his capacity for wine and spirits. *(Enter Durdles with Deputy in tow)* He is wending his way towards an important assignation—

DURDLES: What's that you say, Bill?

CHAIRMAN: An assignation . . . with Mayor Sapsea, who lives just around behind—

DURDLES: What's that you say, Bill?

CHAIRMAN: I said "arround behind."

DURDLES: And so have you!

(Drum comment)

CHAIRMAN: Ladies and gentlemen, essaying the role of Durdles, the Clown Prince of the Music Hall Royale, I give you (and I don't want him back) . . .

DURDLES: You won't get me back. Not at these wages. Ladies and gentlemen, may I make so bold as to introduce my own lad, who'll be playing the part of Deputy tonight, young Nick Cricker, following in his old dad's footsteps.

(Time-step bows)

CHAIRMAN: Ladies and gentlemen, Nick Cricker and Son! Durdles and Deputy await the arrival of Mayor Thomas Sapsea as he returns to his home in—Cloisterham High Street!

(High Street fanfare as curtain opens and townspeople greet each other. As fanfare concludes, they extend their arms towards the wings where Sapsea is supposed to enter. He doesn't. An awkward moment. Throttle, the Stage Manager, has a hurried word in Chairman's ear)

CHAIRMAN: . . . really? With a sack of what? Well, it's unacceptable, isn't it? But you'll notice once again who gets saddled with the— *(To audience)* Ladies and gentlemen, your kind indulgence for a short announcement: The part of Mr. Thomas Sapsea will not, I repeat, will not be portrayed tonight by Mr. James Hitchens, as is stated in your programme. Mr. Hitchens, as many of you already know, has tended to appear more frequently at the bar in the rear than here in front of the footlights. Therefore, it will come as no surprise to our regulars that Mr. Hitchens is once again Massively Indisposed, due to injuries he received while fighting for a lady's honour. *(Pause)* Apparently the lady wished to keep it. And so his part will be portrayed this evening by your own humble chairman and obedient servant —I refer of course, ladies and gentlemen, to myself—Mr. William Cartwright! I hope you are pleased with this last-minute substitution? *(He begs for applause)* And, I might add, it's more *your* luck than mine.

DURDLES: Afternoon, your lordship, sir.

SAPSEA: Good afternoon, Durdles.

DURDLES: Begging your pardon if I sound all dry in the throat, sir. I've a touch of the "tombatism."

SAPSEA: You mean "rheumatism."

DURDLES: No, I mean "tombatism." I've been working on your dead wife's grave!

(Drum comment)

SAPSEA: I'd prefer you to refer to the late Mrs. Thomas Sapsea as just that, Durdles: "the late Mrs. Thomas Sapsea." That is how I like to refer to her; indeed, that is how I like to *think* of her, the late Mrs. Thomas Sapsea. Is her tomb ready?

DURDLES: Yes, guv'nor, the door is all ready for my inscribing. She'll be happy down there under the Cathedral, it's not at all damp, and the moles won't be able to get at her for ages, though there's nothing much you can do about the worms, I mean, they're going to make a meal of Mrs. Sapsea no matter—

CHAIRMAN: That's quite enough, Durdles. *(Regards Deputy)* And who is this—this thing, this boy?

DURDLES: My protege,* squire? Name of Deputy.

DEPUTY: I put the lock on your wife's crypt myself, your lordship.

DURDLES: That's right, I have the key right here *(Displays a ring of keys)*, And it'll be my pleasure to unlock that door

* Rhymes with "siege."

and *slide* your old woman right in there tomorrow, there's room enough for all the royal family to have afternoon tea—

SAPSEA: Yes, yes—

DURDLES: That crypt is a national treasure, if I may make so bold, your grace; just a while ago, Mr. Jarsper asked if I'd take him down into the crypts to see it.

SAPSEA: *(As Chairman. Lighting change; to audience, pointedly)* Now that sounded suspiciously like a clue to me. You may wish to keep track of these suspicious statements.

DURDLES: Steady on, Bill, we don't want the people leaping to conclusions without all the facts at hand! *Otherwise, they'll be running* OFF TO THE RACES!

(A song cue if ever there was one, a vamp commences)

FLO: *(From the side of stage)* Right! Let's have a chorus of "Off to the Races"!

CHAIRMAN: No, no, I'm sorry, Flo, but that song is scheduled for later in the performance. We mustn't do anything that would interrupt the dramatic momentum we're building here. For now we must travel, for reasons that will soon be made clear, to the wickedest corner of the wickedest hole in the fabric of the city of London. Below the street, and beneath contempt, lies the Opium Den of the Princess Puffer!

(Sinister oriental fanfare as we see a chamber of smoke, filled with cheap iron beds and a bizarre mix of discarded furniture and statuary. Comatose bodies lie about, illuminated by a ghastly light that reflects off the Thames and seeps through barred windows located in the high ceiling. Seated in a seedy

armchair is a crone of indeterminate age. She is obviously the proprietress of the establishment and, while sipping gin from a nearby bottle, she alternates between mixing long clay pipes and issuing unpleasant hacking noises)

CHAIRMAN: Here the universal tongue of Opium is spoken, with its subdialects of prostitution, burglary, violence for profit, and murder. And reigning supreme over this blemish on England's fair complexion is the Princess Puffer, who ministrates to her client's needs and who hears more than she tells . . . portrayed this evening by the Grand Dame of the Music Hall Royale, the Queen Mother of the Red Light District . . . that good woman of ill-repute . . . your very own and beloved Miss Angela Prysock!

(Puffer makes her way towards audience as Purcell cues a leading chord)

"THE WAGES OF SIN" (Princess Puffer)

PRINCESS PUFFER:
"CRIME DON'T PAY!" THAT'S WOT I TELLS 'EM.
IF IT DID, WOULD I BE HERE?
MIXING PIPES, WOT THEN I SELLS 'EM
FOR A PINT OF ROTTEN BEER.
THROATS YOU CUT TO POCKET THRUPPENCE,
OR YOU SLUT TO COP SOME SLEEP.
BASH A FACE FOR BLEEDIN' TUPPENCE . . .
PURE DISGRACE TO WORK SO CHEAP.

SO I SAY, DON'T BE A SINNER
FOR THE PRICE OF LONDON GIN.
YOU CAN'T PAY FOR ONE SQUARE DINNER
WITH THE WAGES OF SIN.
SELL MY SOUL? 'COR LOVE, COME OFF IT!

WHO WOULD BUY THIS SACK OF SKIN?
ON THE WHOLE, THERE AIN'T MUCH PROFIT
IN THE WAGES OF SIN, IN THE WAGES OF SIN.
IN THE WAGES OF SIN!

(Prysock/Puffer interrupts her performance to address a gentleman she spots on a box seat)

PRYSOCK/PUFFER: *(To gentleman)* 'Allo, love. Fancy seeing you two nights in a row? What piece of crumpet you been buttering up instead of me? What little slice of raspberry tart— Oh, beggin' your pardon, Miss, I'm sure. First time out on the town with him, is it? Eh? Never you fear, love— I've had him on numerous occasions and whatever he's got in mind, praise god, it'll be over within an instant. (Violinist plays introductory arpeggio, which, in the heat of the moment, becomes an extended cadenza. Prysock approaches him and enquires:) What do they pay you, love? By the note? *(She indicates violinist to audience)* I had him when he was fourteen, god love him. *(To violinist)* You've not had better since, have you? *(To audience)* He's not had *any* since! *(She slips back into Puffer character)*

PRINCESS PUFFER:
I'VE SEEN GIRLS FROM GUTTER FAMBLIES
TRAP RICH MEN WIV FLUTTERY WAYS,
AND THEY COO, "COR, PASS THE JAM PLEASE,"
OVER NUPTIAL BREAKFAST TRAYS.
OVER THERE, IN BED ELEVEN, SLEEPS A BLEEDIN' HYPOCRITE.
SPENDS HIS DAYS EYES CAST TO 'EAVEN:
SPENDS ODD NIGHTS AMONG THIS—
WELL . . .
'S WHY I SAY, DON'T TAKE HALF-MEASURES.
DO THINGS RIGHT AND DIG RIGHT IN!

IN THIS WORLD, THERE'S GREATER TREASURES
THAN THE WAGES OF SIN.
I GET THREATS, BUT SELDOM OFFERS;
IF I DID, I'D PACK IT IN.
YOU CAN'T FILL THAT MANY COFFERS
WITH THE WAGES OF SIN—
(She calls to the back rows) Give your old love some help with the last line now, sing:

ALL:
WITH THE WAGES OF SIN.

PUFFER: Oh, you can do better than that! Get off your bums and give us the notes:

ALL:
WITH THE WAGES OF SIN!!

PUFFER: God love you, I'm sure!

(She blows kisses to all and resumes her seat. Eerie music starts softly)

CHAIRMAN: Miss Angela Prysock, ladies and gentlemen. The meanest room in London! And as the light of day steals into the room, would not the parishioners of Cloisterham be astounded to discover, in Bed Eleven, the goodly choirmaster of Cloisterham Cathedral . . . *(Shooting bolt upright from beneath the blanket of the bed nearest the audience, his eyes quite wild, is)* Mr. John Jasper!

JASPER: Woman! I need laudanum wine, and quickly . . . My task is only half finished and your medicine is less potent than usual.

PUFFER: *(Gets up to prepare laudanum)* Laudanum! So you're mixing opium with wine these days. I'll fix it for you now.

JASPER: Yes, Yes. Before I can get to the changes of colors and great landscapes, I must be rid of him.

PUFFER: Who?

JASPER: *(Sees Shadow of Drood)* Him! Him! *(Drinks offered wine)*

PUFFER: God spare you, there's no one there.

JASPER: There he is! *(Sees Shadow of Jasper)* And there *I* am!

PUFFER: Yes, yes, of course. Now be still and have yourself a pleasant journey.

(Music continues eerily)

"JASPER'S VISION" Ballet

(Puffer resumes her seat as two opium smokers begin a languid sinuous struggle to the death, as if each end of the same snake were trying to choke the other. Jasper watches in fascination as a real murder transpires. The other denizens of Puffer's moan orgiastically as opium smokers rise from their cots like spirits resurrected. Succubae pour from the bed, garbed in outré and, for the period, revealing costumes. Jasper incantates as we share his vision)

JASPER: . . . quickly, more laudanum or she will fade . . . Rosa . . . Rosa Bud! *(As he cries out her name, all music and dance cease and Puffer starts visibly. He mumbles)* Rosa . . . Rosa Bud . . . Rosa . . .

PUFFER: What did you say? Rosa Bud? Did you say Rosa Bud?

JASPER: *(Completely changed)* I can't seem to recall what I said. Could you please direct me to the railway station? I seem to be lost.

PUFFER: Five and thruppence you owes me.

JASPER: That seems a large sum for a small courtesy. However, if you are that needy . . . *(He pays her)* And the railway station?

PUFFER: The nearest is in Aldgate, ten minutes of a walk away from the river.

JASPER: I thank you. *(He looks around)* Incredible.

(He exits. Puffer looks after him)

PUFFER: Who are you then? And *what* are you? *(She turns to exit)*

CHAIRMAN: You might wish to add that line to your list of suspicious statements. Might we have it again, my dear? Yes, once more please.

(Puffer returns to her position)

PUFFER: Who are you then? And *what* are you? . . .

CHAIRMAN: Yes, what indeed. It is now late the next day and as we return to the less sordid confines of Cloisterham the seeds of rivalry are already producing a venomous crop.

(Cloisterham once again. Crisparkle is chatting amiably with Rosa and Drood and spots the Landless twins, who themselves are taking a stroll down Cloisterham High Street)

CRISPARKLE: Ah, and in fact there they are now! Helena! Neville! Allow me to introduce our dear Rosa's betrothed: young Edwin Drood.

DROOD: Sir!

NEVILLE: Sir! I congratulate you on your good fortune, Mr. Drood.

DROOD: Good fortune, sir?

NEVILLE: Your betrothal, sir.

DROOD: *(Realizing)* Oh, Rosa.

CRISPARKLE: Our young Ned is soon to depart himself for your segment of the globe, Neville.

NEVILLE: Ceylon, Mr. Drood?

DROOD: No, but much the same. Egypt.

NEVILLE: Oh, to make your future, sir?

DROOD: No, to ensure that Egypt has one. I shall shortly be taking over my family's engineering concern there, and I plan to pull off a miracle . . .

NEVILLE: Pray, what miracle?

DROOD: The Cairo Transverse, Mr. Landless! A thoroughfare for commerce and coach travel across the desert to Alexandria.

HELENA: A monumental task, Mr. Drood!

DROOD: Yes, Miss Landless.

HELENA: One wonders from where one will obtain, for example, the paving stones?

DROOD: From the pyramids!

NEVILLE: No!

DROOD: My studies show there is enough rock in the top half of the Great Pyramid alone.

NEVILLE: This is English blasphemy! Is it not enough that you take our delicate brew of tea leaves and likewise improve *it* by pouring cow's milk into the—

CRISPARKLE: Neville, please—let's not raise our voices here in —ehm—*(Checks the set to see where he is)* Cloisterham High Street.

DROOD: I mean no offense, sir.

NEVILLE: I did not mean my awkward ways to arouse such emotion, or to ruffle your splendid feathers, Miss Bud.

ROSA: I'm sure Mr. Landless only feels passionately about his part of the world, Edwin.

DROOD: As long as he keeps his passions in check.

NEVILLE: I fear I have not yet adapted myself to your restrained climate. You might forgive me if you knew, yourselves, the warm and uncivilized allure of our homeland.

"CEYLON" (Helena, Neville, Drood, Crisparkle, and Ensemble)

HELENA:
CEYLON . . . CEYLON
BY THE BENGAL BAY . . .

NEVILLE:
EAST OF JAIPUR,

HELENA:
WEST OF MANDALAY . . .

HELENA AND NEVILLE:
AGRA . . . PATNA . . .
SHOLAPUR AND KOLHAPUR AND ALL!
HOW FAR . . . THEY ARE

HELENA:
FROM THE HIGH STREET AND THE MARKET HALL!

DROOD:
IT'S ALL VERY WELL FOR YOU
TO SPEAK OF THIS DISTANT VIEW,
BUT ROSA, WHAT'S PLANNED FOR ME
IS GRANDER THAN SAND AND SEA.
THIS VISTA WITHIN MY SIGHT
WHERE I'LL SET THE WORLD ARIGHT
AWAITS ME—
IT DOMINATES ME.

DROOD:	COMPANY:
IT'S PERFECTLY FINE FOR THEM	CEYLON,
TO SING OF THEIR MINOR GEM,	CEYLON,
BUT THERE IS A ROLE FOR ME,	'CROSS THE INJUN SEAS!
A GOAL I INTEND TO SEE,	T'WARDS THE
A VISION THAT'S IN MY SIGHT—	FJORDS OF
A SCENE THAT'S CLEAN AND	THORNABY-ON TEES!
BRIGHT BEFORE ME!	
YOU CANNOT IGNORE ME.	

DROOD:	HELENA AND NEVILLE:
I WILL SOON BE	MONSOONS,
SHAPING, MOLDING,	TYPHOONS
HOLDING FORTUNE	BREAK UPON THE
IN MY HAND AND	COAST OF MALABAR!
I'LL IMPROVE AND	QUAKING!
SHAKE AND MOVE AND	SHAKING!
CHANGE THE LAY AND	
NATURE OF THE LAND!	CHANGE THE WAY YOU ARE, HEY!

ENSEMBLE AND NEVILLE, HELENA, AND ROSA:
CEYLON, CEYLON,
BY THE BENGAL BAY.
EAST OF JAIPUR,
WEST OF MANDALAY . . .

HELENA:
HOW WARM ARE THE WINDS OF OUR GOLDEN ISLE,

NEVILLE:

HOW COOL ARE THEIR WINDS AND HOW COLD IS THEIR SMILE:

BOTH:	ENSEMBLE AND BRITISH:
THEY WISH US GONE!	THEY'VE BECOME A
WE'LL BE BACK SOMEDAY	THREAT STRAIGHT FROM
CEYLON!	CEYLON!

ALL:

SAIL ON, TO CEYLON!

(Jasper and Sapsea enter towards the end of the song. As Neville and Helena exit, and as townspeople drift away:)

JASPER: You see, Mayor Sapsea? It's just as I've been saying—there is an instinctive rivalry between my own dear boy and this Landless fellow . . . and I fear his hot-blooded Eastern temperament.

SAPSEA: Oh, I think you exaggerate the matter, Mr. Jasper.

JASPER: You have not heard him speak as I have, sir. There is something of the tiger in his blood. I have seen him murderous in his wrath.

SAPSEA: He strikes me as being a troubled but essentially well-meaning boy.

JASPER: *(Howling with frustration)* I will go mad! Do you not realize there is more than one side, one face to all things in nature?

SAPSEA: But really, sir—

JASPER: Beneath Neville's tainted English accent and adopted English manners, there is a heathen Landless, a tribesman Landless, a half-blooded, half-bred half-caste who would kill as easily as he would comb his sleek hair!

SAPSEA: Come now, Mr. Jasper, this is quite extraordinary—

JASPER: *(Almost frothing)* To the contrary, nothing could be more ordinary, sir. *(Suddenly calm)* I myself suffer from this sort of duality on occasion. Sometimes I will . . . forget things . . . and in going back to fetch them, I half-expect to meet myself rounding a corner I've already turned . . .

(Musical vamp begins)

SAPSEA: *(To audience as Chairman)* And what about me, having to be Chairman of this caper and this Sapsea bloke at the same time? It's damned confusing. I assure you.

JASPER: . . . indeed, like our two-sided Neville Landless, I find that . . .

"BOTH SIDES OF THE COIN" (Jasper and Chairman)

JASPER:

I AM NOT MYSELF THESE DAYS.
FOR ALL I KNOW, I MIGHT BE YOU.
THERE'S MORE THAN ROOM ENOUGH FOR TWO INSIDE MY MIND!

SAPSEA:

I AM LIKEWISE IN A HAZE

OF WHO I AM FROM SCENE TO SCENE;
WHAT'S MORE, WE TWO, (WE *FOUR,* I MEAN), ARE IN A BIND!

JASPER:
FOR IS IT, I OR IS IT ME?

SAPSEA:
AND IF I'M HIM *AND* IF I'M HE,
EACH ONE OF US MIGHT NOT AGREE ON WHAT TO DO.

JASPER:
AND IF I TAKE OPPOSING SIDES
WITHIN MYSELF, THEN WHO DIVIDES
UP WHAT IS RIGHT OR WRONG?

SAPSEA:
I'LL GO ALONG WITH YOU.

BOTH:
HA'PENNY, ONE PENNY, TUPPENNY, THRUPPENNY,
TWELVE TO A SHILLING, TWICE THAT TO A FLORIN,
AND WOULD YOU NOT FANCY THE CURRENCY FOREIGN
TO FIND THE SAME FACE ON BOTH SIDES OF THE COIN?
BOB IS YOUR UNCLE FROM PENNIES TO GUINEAS,
THE TWO-SIDED MINT IS THE RULE, NOT EXCEPTION,
AND WOULD YOU NOT FEEL QUITE THE FOOL OF DECEPTION
TO FIND THE SAME FACE ON BOTH SIDES OF THE COIN?

SAPSEA:	JASPER:
ODDS OR EVENS,	HEADS OR TAILS,
IT'S HIGH OR LOW,	OR BLACK OR WHITE,
IT'S UP OR DOWN,	OR LEFT OR RIGHT,
OR NIGHT,	OR DAY!

SAPSEA:
NATURE SELDOM EVER FAILS TO MOST OBLIGINGLY PROVIDE
AN UNDISCLOSED OPPOSING SIDE TO ONE'S DISMAY.

JASPER:
THERE'S SHADOWS IN THIS SHINING MORN,

SAPSEA:
IF THERE'S A ROSE IT BEARS A THORN.

JASPER:
YOU'RE GOOD AS DEAD AS SOON AS BORN,

BOTH:
AND YET WE SMILE.

SAPSEA:
BUT LUCK'S DIVISION IS PERVERSE,

JASPER:
IT SEEMS TO WORK MORE IN REVERSE:

SAPSEA:
IF THINGS ARE BETTER, THEY'LL BE WORSE IN JUST
A WHILE.

BOTH:
HA'PENNY, ONE PENNY, TUPPENNY, THRUPPENNY,
TWELVE TO A SHILLING, TWICE THAT TO A FLORIN,
AND WOULD YOU NOT FANCY THE CURRENCY FOREIGN
TO FIND THE SAME FACE ON BOTH SIDES OF THE COIN?
BOB IS YOUR UNCLE FROM PENNIES TO GUINEAS,
THE TWO-SIDED MINT IS THE RULE, NOT EXCEPTION,
AND WOULD YOU NOT FEEL QUITE THE FOOL OF DECEPTION

TO FIND THE SAME FACE ON BOTH SIDES OF THE COIN?
BOTH SIDES OF THE COIN! HEY! !

JASPER:
HA'PENNY, ONE PENNY, TUPPENNY, THRUPPENNY,
TWELVE TO A SHILLING, TWICE THAT TO A FLORIN,
AND WOULD YOU NOT FANCY THE CURRENCY FOREIGN
TO FIND THE SAME FACE ON BOTH SIDES OF THE COIN?
BOB IS YOUR UNCLE FROM PENNIES TO GUINEAS,
THE TWO-SIDED MINT IS THE RULE, NOT EXCEPTION,
AND WOULD YOU NOT FEEL QUITE THE FOOL OF DECEPTION
TO FIND THE SAME FACE ON BOTH SIDES OF THE COIN?
BOTH SIDES OF THE COIN!

JASPER AND SAPSEA:
HA'PENNY, ONE PENNY, TUPPENNY, THRUPPENNY,
TWELVE TO A SHILLING, TWICE THAT TO A FLORIN,
AND WOULD YOU NOT FANCY THE CURRENCY FOREIGN
TO FIND THE SAME FACE ON BOTH SIDES OF THE COIN?
BOB IS YOUR UNCLE FROM PENNIES TO GUINEAS,
THE TWO-SIDED MINT IS THE RULE, NOT EXCEPTION,
AND WOULD YOU NOT FEEL QUITE THE FOOL OF DECEPTION
TO FIND THE SAME FACE ON BOTH SIDES OF THE COIN?
BOTH SIDES OF THE COIN!
HEY!

SAPSEA: You've convinced me, Mr. Jasper. I shall keep my eyes carefully fixed upon this Neville Landless!

JASPER: A brilliant and original idea, Mayor Sapsea! But now I must—change. Good day, sir . . .

SAPSEA: Bye-bye! *(Then, as Chairman)* Ladies and gentlemen, let us now descend into darkness in hopes of shedding new light upon our curious story . . . as we find ourselves . . . in the crypts of Cloisterham Cathedral!

(With a musical shiver, we see a chamber within the crypts. Labyrinthian corridors are implied. To our left, the prominently-labelled tomb of Mrs. Thomas Sapsea. With the classic creak and ominous rasp of marble drawn across granite, the door to Mrs. Sapsea's mausoleum slowly opens with horrific portent. Light from within the vault seeps out and better illuminates the crypts. At last, Jasper emerges from the mausoleum, a lantern in his hand. With a forceful display of inner strength, he closes the door to the mausoleum and, as the vault seals shut, listens with satisfaction to the repeated reverberations it creates)

JASPER: *(In a near-whisper)* Durdles? Durdles? ?

(Jasper sets the lantern on the floor, and as the light grows, we see Durdles lying semi-comatose near the foot of a stone staircase. Jasper holds up Durdles' ring of keys and removes a single key. He is suddenly startled to hear a distinctly different sound from above. He whirls about towards the staircase and watches in terror as a macabre, distended shadow twists its way down the staircase)

DEPUTY: Durdles! Durdles! Hello? Who's there? Mr. Jarsper . . .

(Stepping from the shadows, Jasper seizes Deputy violently)

JASPER: *(Violently)* What, have you been watching me, you cunning devil? I'll have the blood of you . . . *(Jasper's wild rage endows him with almost inhuman strength and he easily dominates the boy. Deputy, held by the throat, goes limp as if dead. Jasper stands over him breathing heavily)* There. That will serve you.

DURDLES: You murdered him!

JASPER: What? What do you say?

DURDLES: Murder! Murder!

(Jasper's voice and demeanour is suddenly and completely changed. He bends over the boy deeply concerned. His ear to Deputy's chest)

JASPER: Don't be insane, Durdles. Stop talking such lunacy and help me revive the dear boy. I only pray that—oh!

(The "dear boy," who has been faking, kicks out, landing a blow to Jasper's stomach)

DEPUTY: There, you barstard, and I'll stone yer eyes out next time, so help me!

DURDLES: *(Cuffing Deputy)* Quiet, you young wretch!

JASPER: *(Gasping for breath)* Why do you assault me this way, Deputy?

DEPUTY: *(To Durdles)* You're ripe for the asylum, Mr. Jarsper!

(He rushes up the stairs. The bells of the Cathedral's clock tower slowly begin the full toll of three o'clock)

JASPER: Peculiar lad.

DURDLES: Three of a morning? Well, that was excellent wine you gave me, Mister Jarsper. More potent than I'm accustomed. Did you get to look inside Mrs. Sapsea's crypt while I was asleep?

JASPER: No, I seem to have gotten . . . lost.

DURDLES: Oh, well, I was lost myself in a fitful dream, Mister Jarsper. I imagined someone touched me and took something from me—*(He sees his key ring on the floor)* and here's what it was—Fell from me, did you? Mayor Sapsea wouldn't like me leaving the key to his wife's crypt laying about right here in front of her tomb—and now that very same key is missing. What do think, Mr. Jarsper?

JASPER: I think that your world down here still remains somewhat a mystery to me. Come along, Durdles. *(He mounts the stairs)*

DURDLES: *(To audience)* Not so great a mystery as you are to me, Mr. John Jarsper.

(Curtain as Durdles nods ominously. Transitional music)

CHAIRMAN: It is now the very eve of Christmas, but, oh, there is precious little joy in Cloisterham as Edwin and Rosa at last speak words they have long felt.

(Drood and Rosa are strolling by the ruins of Cloisterham)

DROOD: No, Rosa, we are not legally bound to marriage.

ROSA: Then, Eddie dearest, let us change to brother and sister from this day forth.

DROOD: Never be husband and wife?

ROSA: Never.

DROOD: I am honour-bound to confess that this thought does not originate with you alone, Rosa.

ROSA: I know, dear one. You have not been truly happy with our engagement. Nor have I.

DROOD: I am sorry, Rosa.

ROSA: And I for you, poor boy.

DROOD: . . . if only our marriage had not been assured since birth . . . perhaps then we would know how we truly feel towards each other.

"PERFECT STRANGERS" (Drood and Rosa)

ROSA:
IF WE WERE PERFECT STRANGERS,
HOW PERFECT LIFE COULD BE!

DROOD:
I'D KNOW IF I ADORE YOU—
YOU'D KNOW IF YOU LOVE ME.
TOO MUCH WE'VE SEEN TOGETHER TO JUDGE THE VIEW.

ROSA:
TOO MUCH WE'VE BEEN TOGETHER.

DROOD:
AND I ASSUMED THE FUTURE—

ROSA:
AND I PRESUMED THAT YOU WERE THERE . . . AND YET
I'VE WONDERED WHERE WE MET . . . ?

DROOD:
IF WE WERE PERFECT STRANGERS,
I'D FIND MY WAY WITH EASE.

DROOD AND ROSA:
I'D SEE THE PATH BEFORE ME,
THE FOREST FROM THE TREES.

DROOD:
COULD LIFE BE REAL WITHOUT YOU?
YOU'RE ALWAYS THERE.

ROSA:
HOW DO I FEEL ABOUT YOU?

DROOD:
I CARE . . .

ROSA:
. . . TOO NEAR TO TOUCH YOU.
MY DEAREST NED, HOW MUCH YOU MEAN TO ME . . .

DROOD:
BUT ARE WE LOVERS, HOW WOULD WE KNOW IT?
HOW COULD WE FEEL IT? HOW WOULD WE SHOW IT?

ROSA:
HOW MUCH YOU'VE BEEN TO ME . . . .

(As music continues, they speak)

ROSA: Brother.

DROOD: Sister.

ROSA: I pray you will take this clasp . . . left to me by my mother . . . as a vow of my eternal friendship. *(He accepts it)* God bless you.

DROOD: God bless you, dear.

ROSA:
HOW DO I FEEL ABOUT YOU?

DROOD:
I CARE . . .

ROSA:
. . . TOO NEAR TO TOUCH YOU.
MY DEAREST NED, HOW MUCH YOU MEAN TO ME . . .

DROOD:
BUT ARE WE LOVERS, HOW WOULD WE KNOW IT?
HOW COULD WE FEEL IT? HOW WOULD WE SHOW IT?

DROOD AND ROSA:
IF WE'D BEEN PERFECT STRANGERS,
I MIGHT HAVE LOVED YOU PERFECTLY . . .

DROOD: All this will come as a terrible blow to my uncle! *(Rosa turns away in fear)* Why, whatever is the matter?

ROSA: Could we keep our change of plans from Mr. Jasper for a while, Eddy?

DROOD: Yes, of course you're right. Why give him such sad news on Christmas Eve? But now we must be off quickly. He's expecting us for dinner and I fear there's a storm brewing.

(Indeed there is, for we hear a thunderbolt and an ominous rumbling in the clouds. Drood and Rosa hurry off. We are now back where our play started, in the home of John Jasper. Christmas music)

NEVILLE: What a bizarre climate you have here in Cloisterham! First snow and now this threatening storm. The gods must be angry!

CRISPARKLE: *God* must be angry, Neville, not *gods.* We use the singular in England.

(Waiter, later to be identified as Bazzard/Bax, and timorous maids have brought on the dinner table)

HELENA: What a storm for Christmas Eve!

CRISPARKLE: Yes, 'twas like this the night that Rosa's mother died.

HELENA: Neville tells me you were once engaged to Rosa's mother, Mr. Crisparkle?

CRISPARKLE: Yes, yes, but I fear I was a bit too Anglican, a bit too Angular for her taste. *(All freeze; lights and music mysterious as he reflects)* And then, at a seaside party celebrating her second anniversary . . . only a few months after Rosa was born . . . she apparently slipped while walking unobserved along the cliffs, and drowned in the embrace of the ungrateful waves . . . *(End music)* But enough. Let us follow Mr. Jasper's lead and forget our grievances with life and with each other over a sturdy Christmas dinner.

JASPER: I pray you will forgive the meagre merits of my humble table.

(Jasper admits Drood and Rosa, the wind howling as they enter)

DROOD: Hallo, all! Sorry we're late but we fought the storm all the—

NEVILLE: Miss Bud, it is wondrous to see you again.

DROOD: *(Hands Neville his coat)* I had no idea you had taken on domestic staff, Uncle.

ROSA: Edwin! Mr. Landless will take you seriously.

NEVILLE: No fear of that.

JASPER: Now, lads, none of that! Rosa, you've no idea what it means to have you in my chamber.

ROSA: Oh, thank you.

LANDLESS: Miss Bud, how is it that in a season of holly, you remind me of the flowering hibiscus!

DROOD: And how is it you remind me of an inconsistent baker, Neville: for while your metaphors seem quite stale, your manners are uncommonly fresh.

NEVILLE: You go too far, sir!

JASPER: Now, lads, this mulled wine is very good stuff indeed. I Prepared It Specially for you from a recipe I obtained on a recent trip to London.

DROOD: *(Laughs, trying his best)* Well, any port in a storm for me, Uncle!

(Neville accepts a glass)

CRISPARKLE: None for me, thanks.

JASPER: Now let's drink deep.

DROOD: This wine is more potent than usual, Jack.

JASPER: Oh really, I thought you lads would like it. Let's have no more ill will between you!

(They raise their glasses together. Massive thunderbolts)

DROOD: I pledge it, Uncle.

NEVILLE: I so pledge, sir.

WAITER: The goose is cooked and ready, sir!

(All seat themselves at the table)

JASPER: Very good, ladies.

NEVILLE: Miss Bud, I think your next Christmas dinner will be in Egypt.

DROOD: My God, Landless, perhaps you should accompany us there. I'm sure Rosa and I could use someone to carry our bags—

NEVILLE: What?

DROOD: Someone better acquainted with a foreign tongue than he is minding his own.

"NO GOOD CAN COME FROM BAD" (Neville, Rosa, Helena, Drood, Crisparkle)

NEVILLE:
SIR, I DON'T MUCH LIKE YOUR TONE,
THAT SUPERCILIOUS SNEER YOU WEAR!
CLEAR, YOU WEAR A FINER CUT
THAN MINE, AH BUT
A WAISTCOAT WORN
CAN SOON BE TORN,
AND FAGGOTS, TOO,
'TILL MAGGOTS FEED ON YOU!

ROSA: *(Turns to audience, asides)*
SOMETHING IN THIS SPEECH SEEMS OMINOUS TO ME!

HELENA:
TWIN, DON'T OVER-REACH, PRAY PROMISE THIS TO ME!

CRISPARKLE: *(Standing to offer grace)*
PRAISE TO HIM, DIVINE, FOR THIS WE SHOULD BE GLAD.

JASPER:
WON'T YOU TRY SOME WINE?

ALL:
NO GOOD CAN COME FROM BAD!

JASPER: *(Rising, sings to tune of "Two Kinsmen" as he refills their glasses)*
MY DEAREST NEPHEW NED,
I WISH TO WISH YOU WELL!
THE WORLD IS YOURS BEFORE YOU
JUST LIKE—

WAITER: *(Bellows)* Oysters on the shell! *(He and maids bring in a tray of oysters)*

DROOD: *(Retorts to Landless)*
LANDLESS (AS YOU ARE AND KNOWN),
YOUR BLOOD IS HOT BUT LESS THAN PURE!
LESS, I'M SURE, THAN WE.
YOUR HISTORY
WOULD INDICATE THE PAST
OF SOME HALF-CASTE
RUNS THROUGH YOUR VEINS,
YOUR CRUDENESS THUS EXPLAINS.

ROSA:
SOMETHING SENDS A CHILL LIKE FEET UPON MY GRAVE!

HELENA:
CAN MY STRENGTH AND WILL COMPLETELY NEVILLE SAVE?

CRISPARKLE:
COULD THESE WORDS THEY SAY BRING HARM UPON THE LAD?

JASPER:
NIGHT MUST FOLLOW DAY!

ALL:
NO GOOD CAN COME FROM BAD!

(Jasper taps side of water glass to announce toast)

JASPER:
MY DEAREST, DEEPEST FRIENDS!
MAY I PROPOSE A TOAST:

TO ROSA BUD AND EDWIN DROOD,
THREE CHEERS—

WAITER: *(Bellows)* And 'ere's the roast!

(He wheels in the goose on a carving cart. As Drood and Neville approach face-off across this handsome bird, Crisparkle admires the repast)

CRISPARKLE:
HOW VERY BLESSED ARE WE,
WHEN OH SO MANY STARVE!
THY KINGDOM COME, THY WILL BE DONE—

JASPER: *(Enquiring of Neville and Drood)* Which one of you will carve?

(Drood pulls the carving knife savagely from the bird, likewise Neville the carving fork. They almost cross swords as they sing. They are both thoroughly drunk)

NEVILLE AND DROOD:
GLANCES CUT LIKE BLADE THROUGH BONE,
WITH DAGGERS DRAWN I GLARE AT YOU,
THERE AT YOU WHO DARE PRESUME
TO STARE AT WHOM
I'D MAKE MY WIFE
AND SHARE MY LIFE—
I'D SEE YOU DEAD
BEFORE SWEET ROSA WED.

HELENA:
FATE WAITS NEAR!
I FEEL IT, I FEAR IT.

WE ARE FRIENDS, AND YET,
THEY'LL NOT SOON FORGET
HEARING NEVILLE'S THREAT,
EVERY EPITHET!

CRISPARKLE:
IN YOUNGER DAYS, I HUNGERED FOR ANOTHER:
ROSA'S MOTHER!
AFTER ROSA'S BIRTH, SHE LEFT THIS EARTH,
NOW DUST IS ALL I'M WORTH.

ROSA:
SO LONG A TIME,
THEY'VE THOUGHT THAT I'M
A DRESDEN DOLL,
QUITE NAÏVE,
BUT I PERCEIVE
THESE BOYS, THIS NOISE
MORE FRIGHT'NING THAN THEY MIGHT CONCEIVE.

(All repeat their suspicious verse with addition of:)

JASPER:
AND AS I
STAND BY,
TAKE NOTE:
YOUR THROAT
SOUNDS QUITE DRY,
THIS WINE SHOULD SATISFY.

ALL:
WITH THESE NEW ADDITIONS, THERE MAY BE REVEALED
MURDEROUS ADMISSIONS OTHERWISE CONCEALED.

NEVILLE AND DROOD:
FIE ON YOU, I CURSE! FULL WARNING YOU HAVE HAD!

HELENA AND ROSA:
BAD MUST LEAD TO WORSE,

ALL:
NO GOOD CAN COME FROM BAD!
NO GOOD—
NO GOOD CAN COME FROM BAD!

(Music continues under as thunderstorm builds outside)

JASPER: Now, lads, this is Christmas Eve and I will not tolerate any further un-Christian behavior. Ned . . . I implore you.

ROSA: As do I, Edwin.

DROOD: There is no longer any cause for rivalry between us, Neville. You have my friendship . . . if you wish it.

NEVILLE: Then a Merry Christmas to you, Edwin.

(They shake hands, and again, thunder as Jasper pours wine)

DROOD: What a storm for Christmas Eve! I must stroll down to the River Weir to see this fit of nature unchecked. Will you excuse me, Uncle?

JASPER: Of course.

NEVILLE: I will join you on your walk.

(Thunder)

ROSA: *(Moving towards the door)* And we must retire to the Nun's House before the storm . . . Good night, Edwin . . .

DROOD: My dear.

ROSA: *(Quick glance at Neville)* Everyone.

JASPER: Rosa.

HELENA: *(Joining Rosa)* Be careful how you tread, Neville.

CRISPARKLE: *(Similarly)* Well, I shall see the ladies safely home.

(Rosa, Helena, Crisparkle exit)

DROOD: Will you join us, Uncle?

JASPER: No, Edwin, I have plans I must . . . execute. But I will not let you go in that flimsy coat—you shall wear my own humble but serviceable *caped coat!*

(Sinister and significant musical sting. Jasper helps Drood on with coat as Neville calls from doorway)

NEVILLE: Come, Edwin, Destiny awaits!

DROOD: Then good-bye, Uncle! Good-bye, all!

(The sky erupts around Drood framed in the door, then he is gone. Music recedes)

CHAIRMAN: When shall these three meet again? When . . . if ever? It is now late the next day, *Christmas* day, to be sure.

The storm is over, but in its wake, there is to be found no trace of young . . . Edwin . . . Drood.

(Curtain opens, and from either side of the stage enters Rosa and Crisparkle)

ROSA: *(Off)* Mr. Crisparkle!

ROSA: Oh, Reverend, I know something terrible has happened to Edwin!

CRISPARKLE: Oh, let us wait until my assistant, Bazzard, reports. You have heard, I'm sure, the sentiment voiced that no news is most certainly *good* news. Ah, here he is now! *(Enter Bazzard, doom-laden)* Bazzard! What news?

BAZZARD: *(Despondent)* No news.

CRISPARKLE: *(With forced cheer)* There, you see? I don't believe you've met my assistant, Bazzard. His chief occupation is in guiding excursion parties around our church. Quite the showman is our Bazzard, though tragically misplaced.

ROSA: Misplaced?

CRISPARKLE: Yes, he carries with him a Secret. Now, Rosa: what do you think Mr. Bazzard has done?

ROSA: Oh dear! Nothing dreadful I hope?

CRISPARKLE: Mr. Bazzard has written a play. A tragedy.

BAZZARD: *The Thorn of Anxiety.*

ROSA: When will it be performed, Mr. Bazzard?

BAZZARD: *(Proudly)* Never!

CRISPARKLE: Sometimes I think Mr. Bazzard has more pride in its lack of support, like a citizen of Greece who prefers the Parthenon in ruin. But I hope to see Mr. Bazzard's work performed some day.

ROSA: I too, Mr. Bazzard.

BAZZARD: I love the theatrical world. But there are many stages beyond the proscenium. I long to play a larger part!

CRISPARKLE: Then, Bazzard, use your enviable creativity to find some accounting for young Ned.

BAZZARD: *(Overacting his little line)* That assignment I eagerly accept! *(He hurries off)*

ROSA: Oh my dear hopeless Edwin! What has become of him?

CRISPARKLE: *(Also aside)* How like her mother she looks! Had the Lord seen fit to smile on me . . . had her mother not married another . . . nor met her death two years later at that pleasure party by the sea . . . I might have been Rosa's—

ROSA: Father! I need your prayers!

(She kneels before him and holds his hand against her face. The steeple bell begins to toll the evening service)

CRISPARKLE: Rise, my child. The Cathedral bell summons me. We shall find strength in the good English service of Evensong.

ROSA: We must pray that Edwin is still among the living.

CRISPARKLE: Let us hope that he is not already keeping company with your—

(The curtains part to reveal Minor Canon Corner, an area just beyond the doors of Cloisterham Cathedral. The stage is aglow in the full bloom of sunset. Rosa and Crisparkle walk off to church together, his arm steadying her. Enter Jasper and Sapsea, neither of whom sees Rosa)

JASPER: . . . and is it not significant, Mayor Sapsea, that Neville Landless was last seen fleeing the district?

SAPSEA/CHAIRMAN: You've convinced me, Mr. Jasper! A secret murderer could indeed be hiding in Cloisterham's most Affectionate Bosom—and all signs do point to young Neville Landless!

JASPER: My thoughts exactly, sir!

SAPSEA: I shall instruct a few strong fellows to bring him here, using whatever force necessary, so that we may question him!

JASPER: You do that, sir!

(Exit Sapsea and Jasper)

TOWNSPERSON NO. 1: We'll find Neville Landless right enough now.

HORACE: And when we find him, we'll educate the coffee-colored swine. Fetch the dogs!

(A "search" ensues. Dogs are heard in background, cries of "There he is!" "Stop, stop I say!" etc., resound. Deputy runs on)

DEPUTY: Mr. Jarsper, Mr. Jarsper!

(Jasper enters from his home)

JASPER: Oh it's you, you little mud sculpture! Now you'll know what happens to boys who cross me—

DEPUTY: No, no, Mr. Jarsper, I'm just doing my job again. I was sent ahead to tell you we've hunted down Neville Landless.

JASPER: Ah. That's good. Does Mayor Sapsea know of this?

DEPUTY: I've got to run and fetch his holiness now. With any luck, we'll have a hanging for Christmas!

(He races off, Left; simultaneously running on Right is Bazzard)

BAZZARD: Oh, Mr. Jasper. Look what I've discovered!

(He shows something in his hand and Jasper angrily grabs it)

JASPER: Why, it's my coat, the one I gave to Edwin last night! It's been torn to ribbons . . . and, blood, oh God, there's his blood on it! Where did you find this?

BAZZARD: Under a rock by the River Weir.

JASPER: *(Without hope)* My dear boy is murdered. I take this oath before you, Bazzard—record it in your memory—that

I will fasten the crime of murder upon the murderer, and that I devote myself to his destruction!

(He exits, sustained only by a mission)

BAZZARD: *(For the benefit of the third balcony)* I shall remember your words, Mr. John Jasper!

(Curtain, which leaves Bazzard and Chairman at the footlights)

CHAIRMAN: *(Scanning the pages of* Drood) And I believe that's it for you this evening, Phillip.

BAX/BAZZARD: That's right, Bill.

CHAIRMAN: Well . . . I mean, it hardly seems worth your coming down from St. Albans each night, does it? *(Bax/Bazzard nods)* You—you seem to specialize in these Narrow parts of late.

BAX/BAZZARD: Not by choice, Mr. Cartwright.

CHAIRMAN: Let's see, in *Julius Caesar* you played the part of . . .

BAX/BAZZARD: A senator.

CHAIRMAN: Ah. So at least you were in for the kill. *(Ponders)* You know, if you think of it, it's rather odd that Charles Dickens created your character at all. Unless of course he had a more promising future in mind for you.

BAX/BAZZARD: That's been my solace in the role, Mr. Cartwright.

CHAIRMAN: Yes, I'm sure. Still, you do understudy Mr. Paget as John Jasper, I note. Surely one of these days—

BAX/BAZZARD: In actuality, Mr. Paget claims never to have missed a performance in his entire career.

CHAIRMAN: Ah. *(Consults his pocket-watch)* Well, Phillip, *(A moment of immense kindness)* we're almost done with this act and our Second Act is considerably shorter in length than the First. Is there, would you have a song ready at hand? *(Asking the audience)* Shall we? Yes, why not indeed?

(Dream of dreams! Bazzard is barely able to contain his trembling emotions)

BAX/BAZZARD: Well, as a matter of happenstance, Mr. Cartwright, I do have, in common with my role this evening, aspirations as an author and have composed a . . . a brief song which I venture to say underscores the dilemma I share with the character of Bazzard I portray. I hesitate to . . .

CHAIRMAN: Come, come! Its title, Mr. Bax.

BAX/BAZZARD: *(As he hands music to Purcell)* What? Oh, uh, "Never the Luck," Mr. Cartwright.

CHAIRMAN: Ladies and gentlemen, an unscheduled diversion in our journey this evening: the debut of an unpublished and perhaps rightfully-unheard composition: Mr. Phillip Bax singing his own "Never the Luck"!

"NEVER THE LUCK" (Bazzard and Company)

BAX/BAZZARD:

NEVER THE LUCK,
AND NEVER THE LEAD,
AND "NEVER YOU MIND," THEY SAY.
IN TIME WE ALL TASTE
THE LIME IN THE LIGHT,
AND I'LL HAVE MY NIGHT SOMEDAY.
STILL . . . EACH PRECIOUS PART
SEEMS OVER AND DONE
BEFORE I'VE BEGUN TO SPEAK.
I CAST OUT MY LINE
AND KEEP MY HAND IN,
BUT I'LL NOT STAND IN THIS WEEK.
SOME STARLESS NIGHT, THEY'LL CALL TOWARDS THE WINGS:
"WHO HERE DANCES AND SINGS?"
THAT'S WHEN YOURS TRULY SPRINGS
AND SEEING ME THEN, THEY WILL CRY, "WHY
"HE KNOWS EACH LINE,
AND EVERYONE'S CUE
WE MUST LET HIM DO THE PART!"
I'LL LEAP CENTER-STAGE,
THE MUSIC WILL PLAY,
I'LL WALTZ MY WAY INTO YOUR HEART!

(And as he sings, a lovely thing happens. The Chairman steals towards the wings and catches the attention of nearby cast members. Janet Conover, adjusting her costume, steps quietly on stage to watch, as does Nick Cricker, who has been reading the racing form with his braces down. Paget enters too, towel tucked in collar, and he views Bazzard with gentle empathy)

THO' EVER I PLAN,
AND EVER I PLOT,
WITH EVER THE PLUCK TO TRY,
I WAIT FOR MY STAR BY FATE TO BE STRUCK—
BUT NEVER THE LUCK HAVE I . . .

COMPANY:
EVER THE HOPE AND EVER THE SCHEME,

COMPANY:	**BAX/BAZZARD:**
AND EVER THE DREAM!	**BUT EVER THE DREAM HAVE I!**

(On applause, Neville Landless is hurled on-stage by Townsperson No. 1 and No. 2, Horace, and other ragged citizens, who kick at him and hurl abuse. But though clearly out-numbered, Neville is holding more than his own; only the intervention of the Reverend Crisparkle ends the struggle)

CRISPARKLE: Master Neville! And you fellows! Enough! Enough now!

(Crisparkle again shows a surprisingly physical side as he separates Landless and his assailants. As the fight breaks up, Deputy races in with Sapsea in tow. Rosa enters fearfully)

DEPUTY: There's your murderer, sir!

NEVILLE: Reverend Crisparkle. What have I done?

CRISPARKLE: Nothing, I'm certain, lad. I'm sure there is some—

HORACE: Landless! Where is Edwin Drood?

(Jasper, who is now wearing a black arm-band, views the proceedings)

NEVILLE: Where is . . . Why do you ask me that way?

JASPER: Because you were the last person in his company, and he is not to be found!

HORACE: Mayor Sapsea, do you wish to question him?

SAPSEA: *(Prodded by Jasper)* Ehm—You left for the river with Edwin Drood at what time?

NEVILLE: I—in all honesty I cannot recall anything of what transpired once Edwin and I reached the river. That was indeed potent wine you poured for us last night, Mr. Jasper!

SAPSEA: What are these bloodstains upon your shirt-front . . . and upon your walking-stick, Mr. Landless?

NEVILLE: I acquired these bloodstains, sir, just now . . . when these men of yours dragged me forcibly back from the countryside where I had been walking.

HORACE: Neville Landless, as acting constable for the district, I place you under arrest.

(Helena enters breathless)

HELENA: Neville! *(She notices his injuries)* How many of them did it take to mar you in this way?

NEVILLE: *(Proudly)* Eight!

HELENA: *(Whirling on Sapsea)* You have an interesting way with the law here in Cloisterham, Mr. Sapsea. And you, Mr. Jasper . . . for days now you have been warning all Cloisterham of impending violence between your nephew and my brother . . . what do you know of all this?

JASPER: Only that my nephew is dead.

CRISPARKLE: Mayor Sapsea . . . I warrant that young Neville has no knowledge of Master Drood beyond that which he has freely volunteered.

HELENA: And you shall volunteer nothing further, Neville.

(Rosa rushes to Helena's side)

SAPSEA: I would remind you and your brother that there is the issue of MURDER at hand—

(Rosa gasps, wavers as if to faint; Crisparkle holds her steady)

HELENA: Before you utter that word again, you laughable man, perhaps you will be good enough to supply a body, a victim, a corpse . . . something more tangible than an errant nephew, a timorous uncle, and a ludicrous city official who has no backing for his charges beyond pure pomp and sheer circumstance.

CRISPARKLE: Hear, hear.

ROSA: Well said, Helena!

CRISPARKLE: She's right, you know, Mr. Sapsea. Without Edwin's body, you cannot possibly arrest young Master Neville.

SAPSEA: Oh, very well, release him.

HELENA: Oh, bless you, Mr. Crisparkle!

(Impulsively, she kisses him on the cheek. He stares in wonderment)

CRISPARKLE: I am overpaid.

HELENA: I only wish I could express my gratitude without this strange, somewhat geographically untraceable accent!

SAPSEA: *(Defeated and deflated)* I must consider matters. Mr. Crisparkle, are you certain . . .

(He walks Crisparkle off. Helena takes Neville upstage and looks at his wounds, comforting him. Deputy and the ruffians confer; other townspeople gossip eagerly. Which leaves Jasper and Rosa downstage. Rosa turns as if to leave and flinches as she sees Jasper staring her down. Though surrounded by others, she is as alone and as frozen as a cobra's selected victim)

JASPER: *(Suavely)* Rosa! We have both been guilty of neglecting your music lessons. When shall we resume?

ROSA: *(Immense courage)* Never, sir.

JASPER: Am I being politely told that you have abandoned your studies altogether?

ROSA: The politeness is yours, not mine. I beg not to be questioned—I will not answer any more. At least I have that in my power.

JASPER: Rosa, I—

ROSA: I do not wish to hear you, sir.

(Jasper smiles and takes her arm, twisting it between her body and his, so that his actions can't be seen by those nearby)

JASPER: I do not forget how many eyes command a view of us. But you shall hear me, even against your wishes. Dearest Rosa. *(Additional unseen pressure. She suppresses a cry of pain)* Charming Rosa. Even when my dear boy was engaged to you, I loved you madly. I hid my—*our* secret loyally, did I not?

ROSA: You were as false to him, sir, daily and hourly, as you are now. You know that you made me afraid to open his kind eyes to the truth . . . that you are a bad, bad man!

JASPER: How beautiful you are! You are more beautiful in anger than repose! I don't ask for your love . . . give me yourself and your hatred, that pretty rage, that enchanting scorn! It will be enough for me. *(She starts to pull away, but he snaps her back)* I warn you, sweet witch, rare charmer, you must stay or do more harm than can be undone.

ROSA: You're mad!

JASPER: I mean to show you how mad my love is—

ROSA: *(Bitterly)* Love! You dare to use that word!

"THE NAME OF LOVE" and "MOONFALL" (reprise)

ROSA:
LOVE IS BUT A WORD THAT WANDERED HERE FROM PASTURES GREEN
WHERE IT WAS RARELY SAID OR SEEN AND SELDOM SUNG.
INNOCENT ENOUGH, IT WAS INTENDED TO BE USED ON RARE OCCASIONS,
NOT ABUSED BY EVERY TONGUE.
RARELY HAS A WORD BEEN EVER TAKEN SO IN VAIN,
WHAT LITTLE MEANING MIGHT REMAIN IS QUICKLY BLURRED.
NEVER HAS THERE BEEN SO QUITE EXHAUSTED SUCH A TERM,
YOUR SIGHS AND SYLLABLES CONFIRM HOW DRAINED THIS WORD.

ROSA:	JASPER:
YOU CALL IT LOVE,	I CALL IT LOVE,
I CALL IT RUDE.	YOU CALL IT RUDE.
I CALL IT LUST!	YOU THINK ME JUST
I CALL IT LEWD.	A BIT TOO CRUDE.
I CALL IT CRUEL.	AND I THE FOOL,
I CANNOT BEAR	YET STILL I DARE
TO CALL IT LOVE!	TO CALL IT LOVE!
I THINK IT FOUL.	I SEE YOU SCOWL,
I THINK IT VILE.	YOU SEE ME SMILE.
NO MORE I'LL TAKE	'TIS YOU I'LL BREAK!
OF CUNNING GUILE!	I'VE NO DENIAL
YOU'RE WORSE THAN BAD:	MY WORDS ARE MAD:
YOU GIVE TO SIN	I SPEAK THEM IN
THE NAME OF LOVE!	THE NAME OF LOVE!

ROSA:
ROSA BUD, THE DAINTY LITTLE FACE WHOSE EVERY CURL

CONFIRMS THAT SHE'S A CHILD, A GIRL, A NEOPHYTE:
ROSA IS THE ONLY SOUL IN CLOISTERHAM, IT SEEMS,
WHO SENSES JUST THE SORT OF DREAMS YOU DREAM AT NIGHT.
DID YOU THINK YOUR STARE WOULD STOP MY SEEING?
EVERY FIBRE OF MY BEING TOLD ME SINCE I WAS BETROTHED
THAT YOUR MOST UNNATURAL ATTENTION CONJURES WORDS I DARE NOT MENTION.
YOU MUST KNOW HOW MUCH I LOATHED

ROSA:

TO KNOW YOUR WANTS,
TO SEE YOU CLUTCH,
TO HEAR YOUR VOICE,
TO FEEL YOUR TOUCH!
A DREADFUL TASK
TO EVEN SPEAK
THE NAME OF LOVE!

JASPER:

YOU KNOW MY WANTS.
I NEED NOT CLUTCH.
YOU HAVE NO CHOICE.
IS IT SO MUCH
FOR ME TO ASK?
I ONLY SEEK
THE NAME OF LOVE!

ROSA:

I WILL NOT FEAR
MY TRAGIC PLIGHT.
I HAVE A CHOICE:
I'LL TAKE TO FLIGHT.
I'LL NOT PERMIT
YOU TO DESECRATE
THE NAME OF LOVE!

JASPER:

I LOVE TO HEAR
THE ANGRY BITE
OF YOUR FAIR VOICE!
ONE BLAZING NIGHT,
YOU WILL SUBMIT
AND GIVE YOUR FATE
THE NAME OF LOVE!

(As they segue into "Moonfall," a bold blood-red moon comes from behind a cloud and illuminates them as the Cathedral bell chimes midnight. Rosa tries to break away from Jasper's hypnotic hold, but is repeatedly drawn back in fascinated terror)

ROSA:	JASPER:
AND IN THE MOONFALL,	AND IN THE MOONFALL,
CAN YOU NOT SEE THIS VICTIM AND LO,	CAN YOU NOT FREE THIS VICTIM YOU SO
HIS SLAVE,	ENSLAVE?
SAVE ME,	SAVE ME,
AND YET HE SEEMS SO IN PAIN!	AND LET THESE DREAMS REMAIN.
JOHN, YOU MAKE ME LIKE STONE,	AWAKE, MY OWN,
TRANSFIXED WITH WONDER,	TRANSFIXED WITH ONE . . .
MIXED WITH THE THUNDER	
OF THIS LOVE.	OF THIS LOVE.
YOU CALL IT LOVE!	MY ALL, MY LOVE,
THE NAME OF LOVE IS CHILLING TO ME!	YOUR NAME IS LOVE AND THRILLING TO ME!

ROSA AND JASPER:

BENEATH THESE SKIES ONE NIGHT UNKNOWN WOULD HE/SHE DARE?
BETWEEN OUR EYES ONE SIGHT ALONE WE SHARE
THE SIGHT OF MOONFALL
AS IT COMES INTO VIEW . . .

ROSA:	JASPER:
SO THAT	SO I PROMISE THAT YOU SHALL BE
SOON I	SOON A GOLDEN IDOL WHOM I
ONLY	OWN AND LOVE AND LEAD INTO A

SEE BUT	SEA OF LIGHT! 'TIS BUT THE FALLING
YOU!	MOON!
SEE BUT YOU!	FALLING MOON!

(She flees; after a moment, he pursues her. Curtain.)

END OF ACT ONE

ACT TWO

(The audience receives no official notice that the Intermission has ended; no bells or buzzers sound, no lights flash. Purcell returns to his podium and leads orchestra in a brief reprise of "There You Are." This should cause at least some members of the audience to assume that something is in the process of commencing, as our Chairman enters)

CHAIRMAN: Ladies and gentlemen, a warm round of applause if you please for our fully-trained orchestra, under the cryptic baton of Mr. Thomas Purcell! *(Purcell bows magnificently)* Pray take your time in resuming your seats, dear friends. *(By now, a majority of the audience has perceptively realized that Act Two is in progress, and the hurried milling-about for seats should add a pleasant air of confused informality to the theatre. Our Chairman gazes down at a straggler in the first few rows)* Don't worry about being the last, madame—it only means that everyone is looking at you. Incidentally, if you're enjoying our modest efforts tonight, I heartily recommend you return to this "venue" next week, when the Music Hall Royale shall premiere its latest and most ingenious work: *Hamlet—Part Two!*

FLO: *(Again, from the wings)* Never mind *Hamlet, Part Two.* Give us "Off to the Races."

CHAIRMAN: I promise you, Flo, before the evening is over, I shall take you all "Off to the Races." *(Rubbing hands in anticipation)* Good enough. We are, I trust, rested, relaxed, restored, renewed, and more than ready to conclude what is certainly the most ambitious endeavour to date of your own Music Hall Royale: that of solving, by your vote, shortly to be counted . . . *(Gavel once)* The Mystery *(Gavel twice)* of Edwin Drood!

(Orchestral flourish and underscore. Lights dim)

CHAIRMAN: *(Fanfare)* Six months have passed! An English summer is in progress. Still there is to be found no trace of young Edwin Drood, and all of Cloisterham is agog with rumor and suspicion. Two Enquiring Sleuths are about to appear on the scene: one being the Princess Puffer, whom you have already met . . . *(Enter Puffer/Prysock, who cheerily acknowledges audience, and exits)* . . . the other being a Detective, a man of mystery who wears a bulky coat, a fulsome beard, and the name of Dick Datchery. *(Enter Datchery, who takes a pipe from mouth and enquires of Chairman:)*

DATCHERY: Eh?

CHAIRMAN: I said, *Dick Datchery!*

DATCHERY: Right. *(Exits)*

CHAIRMAN: These apparent strangers approach with Grand Intentions and Great Expectations—which I might add we shall be presenting in Brighton next season—and like ourselves, Dick Datchery and the Princess Puffer are just now arriving at *Cloisterham Station!*

(Curtain, revealing the London mail train just pulling in to Cloisterham Station. We hear a final shriek from its whistle as, with steam rolling from under the train's carriage, a cross-sampling of English humanity steps from out its doors, most prominent of whom is John Jasper, who is still dressed in mourning and not yet quite "himself." He looks much as he did in Puffer's opium den. As he exits, Dick Datchery and Puffer suddenly step from the train, both staring intently after Jasper)

CHAIRMAN: Ah yes, there's Mr. John Jasper back from another treatment in London. And in his wake note that, among the many curious souls of Cloisterham, none are more intently curious than these two sleuths.

(Datchery is a ragged bundle of a man with long platinum hair and beard, while Puffer is dressed in what, sadly, must be her best clothes. They head downstage simultaneously but oblivious to each other, and though they sing and move in tandem throughout the following number, neither acknowledges the other)

"SETTLING UP THE SCORE" (Datchery and Puffer, with Ensemble)

PUFFER:
HERE TO TRACK THIS MAN IN BLACK AM I,
WITH ONE CLUE AS TO THE WHO AND WHY.

DATCHERY:
I FIND MYSELF
IN THIS AGGRAVATING FORM AND FACE,
GRAVITATING TO THIS PLACE,
NAVIGATING T'WARDS THIS CASE!

PUFFER AND DATCHERY:
I'VE COME TO TOWN, MY EAR AT EVERY DOOR,
HALF THE CLOWN, YET CRAFTY AT THE CORE.
SETTLING DOWN TO SETTLE UP THE SCORE,
A KETTLE FULL OF FISH I'LL FRY,

PUFFER AND DATCHERY:
I'LL COOK EACH GOOSE,
TO MIX A METAPHOR,
AND UNLOOSE A MIGHTY METEOR
SETTLING DOWN TO SETTLE UP THE SCORE,

DATCHERY:
MY METTLE WILL BE MORE THAN TESTED.
A DEBT'LL BE REPAID BEFORE I'VE RESTED—OH!

DATCHERY:
DROOD,

PUFFER:
NO WORD,

DATCHERY:
WHAT'S BREWED,

PUFFER:
NO GRAVE,

DATCHERY:
NO TOMB!

DATCHERY AND PUFFER:
WHO'LL SAY WHO'S DONE WHAT AND WHY TO WHOM?

DATCHERY:
I'M ON THE SCENT. I'M INVENTING EVERYTHING I AM.

PUFFER:
WHERE'S THE SACRIFICIAL LAMB

DATCHERY:
'ERE IN BLOODY CLOISTERHAM?

PUFFER AND DATCHERY:
I'VE COME TO TOWN, MY EAR AT EVERY DOOR:
DID EDWIN DROWN OR WAS HE WASHED ASHORE?
I'M BEARING DOWN TO SETTLE UP THE SCORE,
RED HERRING ON A BRINY BEACH.

I'LL SOLVE THIS YET!
I'M GRAND INQUISITOR.

MAKE A BET
YOU'VE MET ME ONCE BEFORE.
MAKE A THREAT?
I ONLY WISH YOU WOULD.
I'M SETTLING UP THE SCORE FOR GOOD!

(A mysterious vamp continues as we "dissolve" to Cloisterham High Street, Datchery and Puffer exiting on opposite sides of the street. Enter Crisparkle and Sapsea)

SAPSEA: Ah, Reverend, there you are! All things bright and beautiful tonight, don't you think?

CRISPARKLE: Yes, as if the stars were mere punctures in the ceiling of earth, through which heaven's light can be seen. Or something along those lines. *(To audience)* I only wish my assistant Bazzard, *who is away on business,* could see such a night as this!

(All note this and whisper. As Crisparkle and Sapsea go off, enter Durdles and Deputy)

DURDLES: Hold on there, boy! Here's a face we've not seen before! *(As Deputy goes to Puffer, Durdles speaks to Datchery. Underscoring stops under dialogue)* Welcome to fair Cloisterham, Captain. I am in the way of being Official Greeter to all visitors who might have the price of a bottle of wine on them. My name is Durdles.

DATCHERY: My name is Datchery, Dick Datchery, and I was wondering if lodgings could be found in these parts?

(All silent, they listen)

DURDLES: Oh, no doubt, Mr. Datchery.

DATCHERY: Something architectural and out of the way . . . Inconvenient.

DURDLES: Oh, we have any number of inconvenient lodgings here in Cloisterham, sir.

DATCHERY: Close to the Cathedral as well?

SAPSEA: Excuse me, sir, I couldn't help overhearing. The only such accommodation that I know of along those lines is a single lodging just above the rooms of Mr. John Jarsper. He's a great admirer of my own—

DATCHERY: Ah, is that the fellow who has been much afflicted by the loss of his nephew, Edwin Drood?

(Puffer's ears pick up at this)

PUFFER: Wait on, boy! This much afflicted fellow, John Jasper, is he always dressed in mourning these days?

DEPUTY: That's the man, and you won't catch me goin' near him again.

DATCHERY: Why is that, boy?

DEPUTY: 'Cos I ain't going be lifted off my legs and choked again.

DATCHERY: I find that most interesting. I shall enjoy watching the Comings and Goings of this town. *(He exits limping)*

SAPSEA: That man should speak to his tailor.

PUFFER: Here. There's something suspicious about that Mr. Datchery.

DURDLES: *(To Puffer but also to audience)* Steady on your ladyship . . . let's not be leaping to conclusions without the facts at hand!

CHAIRMAN: An excellent point for us all to keep in mind . . . and a statement which brings us, rather adroitly I think, to a song. A merry air which we have woven into the fabric of our story with hardly a seam showing . . . *(Orchestra begins to vamp)* . . . for what evening at the Music Hall Royale would be complete without a rendition of its trademark theme: "Off to the Races"!

"OFF TO THE RACES" (Chairman, Durdles, Deputy)

CHAIRMAN:
QUICK CONCLUSIONS OFTEN LEAD THE BEST OF US ASTRAY.
THE WISEST MOVE IN LIFE IS JUST TO WAIT.
OTHERWISE, OUR GALLOPING EMOTIONS RUN AWAY

CHAIRMAN, DURDLES, AND DEPUTY:
LIKE HORSES AT THE GATE.
OFF TO THE RACES, OFF TO THE RACES,
OFF TO THE RACE WE GO,
BUT WHERE THE CHASE IS AND WHAT THE PACE IS,
WE SELDOM SEEM TO KNOW.

DURDLES:
MEN WITH BROKEN HEARTS HAVE VOWED TO NEVERMORE PURSUE
A MEMBER OF THE SOFT AND SAVOURED RACE.
FIRMLY ANCHORED TO THE GROUND, THEY SUDDENLY WILL VIEW

DURDLES AND DEPUTY:
A FAIR AND FAVOURED FACE.
OFF TO THE RACES, OFF TO THE RACES,
WHEN FLIRTING FACES CALL!

DEPUTY AND CHAIRMAN:
HIS SAVING GRACE IS STRONG DRINK REPLACES
THE NEED FOR LOVE AT ALL.

ALL:
DON'T FALL BACK ON YOUR ASSUMPTIONS,
HASTY PRESUMPTIONS MIGHT DO YOU IN.
MIND THE TRACK. LIKE A NAG RUNNING BLIND,
TRY LAGGING BEHIND:
YOU'LL FIND YOU'LL WIN.

CHAIRMAN:
BLESS OUR QUEEN VICTORIA, SHE'S 'AD NINE KIDS TO DATE.
YOU WONDER HOW PRINCE ALBERT GOT ENTHUSED!
PROBABLY BY HER DECREE HE HAD TO PROCREATE:
SAID SHE, "MAKE ME AMUSED!"

ALL:
OFF TO THE RACES, THE ROYAL RACES,
THE SAME AS POOR FOLK DO.

DEPUTY:
WHEN SHE EMBRACES, HER ROYAL GRACE IS
THE SAME IN WANTS AS YOU.

ALL:
AND THE RACE IS WON BY THE TARDY,
NOT THE FOOLHARDY FOOLS THAT WE BE.
DON'T UNLACE YOUR MADCAP ABANDON,
DO AND YOU'LL LAND UNDONE.
NOT ME!

George Rose as the Chairman, Mr. William Cartwright

George Rose with the Company in ''Off to the Races''

Jerome Dempsey, Joe Grifasi and Stephen Glavin with members of the Company in ''I Wouldn't Say No'' (a song dropped from the show prior to the Broadway opening)

Cleo Laine as Princess Puffer with Howard McGillin and the Company in "The Wages of Sin"

The Chairman and the Suspects: Joe Grifasi, Howard McGillin, Jerome Dempsey, Patti Cohenour, George Rose, Cleo Laine, John Herrara and Jana Schneider

Betty Buckley as Edwin Drood

SO WE CALL UPON YOU ALL TO HOLD YOUR HORSE'S REINS
BEFORE YOU SOLVE THIS DICKENS OF A CRIME.
SOMETIMES HAVING PATIENCE IS AS GOOD AS HAVING BRAINS,
SO TAKE YOUR BLOODY TIME . . .
POUR OUT THE SPIRITS! THE END IS NEAR, IT'S ONLY A LENGTH OR SO!
DON'T BEGIN TO BEAT YOUR TAR OFF FOR THE FINISH ISN'T FAR OFF.
TO THE RACES!
OFF TO THE RACE WE GO . . . TALLY-HO!

PUFFER: Excuse me, ladies, can you tell me where Mr. John Jasper—*(Sees Rosa and, stunned, gasps for breath)*

ROSA: Oh, are you ill?

PUFFER: *(Hiding her face)* No, I'm always this way, Miss.

(Rosa and Helena exit, Puffer recovers)

PRYSOCK/PUFFER: Well, now I have one of the very bits of information I came here for!

DURDLES: Then you're leaving Cloisterham already?

PUFFER: Not bloody likely! I didn't come this far only to turn away with but one piece of puzzle in my hand. *(Easy musical vamp begins)* I've never in my wretched life been this close to getting anything I set about after; more the fool I'd be to pull back, just when I'm winning. I've never understood those in life who ease up—just when they should push on . . .

"DON'T QUIT WHILE YOU'RE AHEAD"
(Puffer and Company)

PUFFER:
ONCE I BET MY LAST TEN PENCE—AND WON.
TWICE AS RICH THEN, FRIENDS SAID, "CALL IT DONE!"
"HOW SAD," I SAID.
"SO THAT'S YOUR WILDEST DREAM, EH, THEN . . .
TWENTY PENCE INSTEAD OF TEN?
DOUBLE UP MY BET AGAIN!"

IN LIFE, WE START THE SAME AS WHEN WE'RE DONE:
IF YOU LOSE, YOU'RE JUST WHERE YOU'VE BEGUN—
IF YOU'VE WON, DON'T QUIT WHILE YOU'RE AHEAD,
JUST PRESS YOUR BLESSED LUCK INSTEAD!

DATCHERY:
DON'T TRY TO THINK WHAT MOVE MIGHT BE BEST.
USE THE HEART THAT BEATS WITHIN YOUR BREAST,
NEVER REST . . . DON'T QUIT WHILE YOU'RE AHEAD.
SING OUT:

DATCHERY AND PUFFER:
"THERE'S MORE IN STORE FOR ME"

BAZZARD AND DURDLES:
I SEE MY DREAM SHIP FIN'LY COMIN' IN
LIKE A STEAMSHIP ANCH'RIN' IN TO WIN

PUFFER AND DATCHERY:
LIFT YOUR CHIN! REMEMBER WHAT I SAID,
DON'T QUIT WHILE YOU'RE AHEAD, LET GO!

ROSA AND HELENA:
I KNOW THERE MUST BE LOVE THAT'S YET TO BE,

ONLY JUST THREE WINKS AWAY FROM ME,
HOPEFULLY . . .

PUFFER, DATCHERY, BAZZARD, DURDLES:
DON'T QUIT WHILE YOU'RE AHEAD,
DON'T WORRY HOW YOU TREAD. WHO CARES?

NEVILLE AND CRISPARKLE:
AND THERE'S MY CHANCE, ONE PIPE-DREAM THAT IS MINE,
A ROMANCE, JUST RIPE UPON THE VINE.

ROSA AND HELENA:
DON'T RESIGN!

NEVILLE, CRISPARKLE, ROSA, HELENA, WENDY AND BEATRICE:
NO VICTOR EVER FLED!

PUFFER, DATCHERY, BAZZARD, DURDLES:
DON'T QUIT WHILE YOU'RE AHEAD TO STAY!

ALL:
TA-RAY-TA-RAH!
BOOM!
BANG IT, BASH IT, HOO-RAY-HA-RAH!
BOOM!
CLANG IT, CLASH IT, OO-LAH-DEE-DAH!
DON'T QUIT WHILE YOU'RE AHEAD,
DON'T SAY, "I'M OFF TO BED, FAREWELL"

JASPER:
FULL WELL I KNOW!
DON'T LET THE MOMENT GO TO WASTE
NOT WITH VIC-T'RY CLOSE ENOUGH TO TASTE

CHAIRMAN AND JASPER:
HEED THE CALL WITH ALL DUE HASTE!

ALL:
FOR GOD'S OWN SAKE!
SO RAISE THE STAKE! YOU STRUCK A LUCKY VEIN,
NEVER BREAK THROUGH ANY LUCKY CHAIN;
THE REFRAIN "DON'T QUIT WHILE YOU'RE AHEAD"
AS EAS-LY DONE AS SAID, YOU'LL SEE:

TA-RAH-TA-REE!
BOOM!
BANG IT, BASH IT, OO, GLORY BE!
BOOM!
CLANG IT, CLASH IT, OO-LAH-DEE-DEE!
DON'T QUIT WHILE YOU'RE AHEAD!
SING OUT, "THERE'S MORE IN STORE FOR ME"

(The song ends. Then reprise)

CHAIRMAN: Encore, Maestro, s'il vous plaît!

ALL:
AND NOW AT LAST, WE SEE THE SLIGHTEST GLIMM'RING OF LIGHT
QUITE SHIMM'RING IN THE DIM, DULL OF NIGHT.
SO LONG HAVE WE BEEN BLIND,
BUT FIN'LLY WE UNWIND THE PLOT.

THE TRUTH IS THIS: WE FIND THAT WE—

(Their voices and the music abruptly cease. Puffer and Datchery look around anxiously; we hear the orchestra members frantically thumbing through their music looking for the next page of score. Jasper/Paget steps out of character and peers in the direc-

tion of the Chairman as if to ask what is going on. The audience may get the uncomfortable feeling that someone has forgotten a line, that Something Has Gone Wrong . . . The play collapses)

CHAIRMAN: *(At last, and with great sadness)* Ladies and gentlemen. It was at this point in our story that Mr. Charles Dickens laid down his pen forever. And so, my dear friends, this is all we shall ever know for sure about the Mystery of Edwin Drood. Tonight, however, at least within the confines of this humble theatre, we shall together solve, resolve, and conclude: *(Gavel once)* The Mystery . . . *(Gavel twice)*

ALL: . . . of Edwin Droooood!

(Final gavel)

CHAIRMAN: One minor mystery we can resolve immediately, though it has little to do with the plot at hand. You see, most literary experts agree that our enquiring Detective, Mr. Dick Datchery, is actually Someone We Have Already Met, a character from Act One who is roaming Cloisterham disguised as Datchery so as to better investigate the disappearance of Edwin Drood. And . . . as many of you have no doubt already guessed, the part of Datchery has been taken thus far this evening by that Master and Mistress of male impersonation: Miss Alice Nutting! *(With a flourish, Datchery twirls off "his" coat, beard, and wig to reveal, in abbreviated costume and tights, a fetching and feminine Miss Alice Nutting)* But this does not mean that Edwin Drood is Datchery. Oh no, far from it. The reason for Miss Nutting's portrayal of Dick Datchery this evening is . . . well . . . is that she was contracted to appear for two acts of this play, and our Management believes in an honest week's work for an honest day's pay, if you catch my drift. Which brings us to our first key question: Is Edwin Drood dead . . . or alive? Mr. Charles Dickens experimented with many different titles for our story, for example:

(In their "own" voices)

NUTTING/DROOD: The Loss of Edwin Drood.

CONOVER/HELENA: The Flight of Edwin Drood.

GRINSTEAD/NEVILLE: The Disappearance of Edwin Drood.

CHAIRMAN: But nowhere the Death or Murder of Edwin Drood. On the other hand, many would say that a Mystery without a Murder is no mystery at all. Tonight, ladies and gentlemen, our questions shall be answered primarily by You. But in a daring and perhaps dangerously democratic move, the Music Hall Royale has decided to grant Our Company Themselves the right to vote upon one issue each night. And so my fellow acolytes of the thespianic persuasion, this evening your question will be . . . ?

STAGE MANAGER: "IS EDWIN DROOD DEAD—OR ALIVE?" Miss Nutting, who has a vested interest in the outcome, will kindly turn her back to the cast. *(Nutting does so, confident of the outcome)* Gentlemen, ladies . . . as your whim takes you this evening. All those who believe Edwin Drood is dead, please raise your hands. Thank you. And all those who believe Edwin Drood is alive, do the same now, if you please.

(Cast members without exception vote Drood dead)

CHAIRMAN: I'm sorry, Miss Nutting, but you've snuffed it. By a massive majority, I fear. *(Nutting/Drood is astounded;*

Cast is pleased. Nutting burns and fumes as Chairman continues) And our next key question, Mr. Throttle?

STAGE MANAGER: "WHO IS THE DETECTIVE DATCHERY?"

CHAIRMAN: Well, we can safely eliminate Edwin Drood from that consideration, since our cast has voted him dead for the remainder of the evening—

NUTTING: *(Finally exploding at Cast and Chairman)* Dead? Ha and Bloody Ha Ha! You absolute, envious little shits! It's obvious to everyone here that Drood—that I am Datchery, and it's even more transparent that this petty, jealous cast bitterly resents the attention I've received in the local press! Good-bye, all!

(Nutting storms off)

CHAIRMAN: Well, I—really, Miss Nutting, I'm sure that . . . *(She is gone. Chairman appeals to audience)* You have no idea the week we've had with her. First her dressing room was too small, then her moustache was too bushy. I said to her, I said, "Miss Nutting, you are splitting hairs!" *(Leers in search of laughter)* Well, please yourselves . . . I must apologize, ladies and gentlemen, for this bit of unpleasantry in what, I'm sure you'll agree, has been an otherwise flawless evening. But in all fairness to our cast and to our story, I must strenuously point out that many, many literary experts disagree with Miss Nutting's contention that Edwin Drood and Dick Datchery are one and the same person. Indeed, there are several prime candidates for the face behind Datchery's beard! For instance, I offer you: Helena Landless! About her, Neville revealed in Act One:

NEVILLE: *(Stepping forward)* "In desperation, Helena tried on more than one occasion to flee our stepfather's cruel and miserly hand, even disguising herself as a boy."

CHAIRMAN: A hit, a palpable hit! But is it a meaningful thrust . . . or misdirection? Wouldn't Helena Landless be fearful of pursuing John Jasper, under the given circumstances?

HELENA: *(Stepping forward)* "Not under any circumstances!"

(Helena and Neville step back)

CHAIRMAN: But the candidates hardly end there. What say you of—Bazzard?

BAZZARD: *(Stepping forward)* "I love the theatrical world. But there are many stages beyond the proscenium. I long to play a larger part."

CHAIRMAN: Who more likely to don such melodramatic garb and seek the spotlight? Why otherwise does he appear in our story at all? Reverend Crisparkle has just recently stated:

CRISPARKLE: *(Stepping forward)* "I only wish my assistant Bazzard, who is away on business, could see such a night as this!"

(He and Bazzard step back)

CHAIRMAN: Why even mention this useless bit of information . . . unless to point at Bazzard—or divert our attention away from: Neville Landless?

NEVILLE: *(Stepping forward)* "From my earliest remembrances, I've been secret and revengeful."

CHAIRMAN: Who more likely to investigate the disappearance of Drood than he who is most suspected of foul play? Or did someone else wish to clear Neville's name?

CRISPARKLE: *(Stepping forward)* "Neville has been entrusted to my care."

CHAIRMAN: The Reverend Mr. Crisparkle, whose passions and energy lay hidden beneath his clerical garb . . . perhaps he has adopted yet another uniform, that of Datchery, to save the lad who has been his charge and responsibility. And then there is the puzzling and intriguing possibility of . . . Rosa!

ROSA: *(Stepping forward)* "I beg not to be questioned—I will not answer any more! At least I have that in my power!"

CHAIRMAN: Could it be that we have underestimated the resourcefulness of this woman-child? Did she take it upon herself to investigate the disappearance of Edwin Drood? Looks can be deceiving.

MALE ENSEMBLE: *(Knowingly)* I'll say! *(Peregrine/Rosa, embarrassed, adopts her most virginal pose)*

CHAIRMAN: This much I do know for certain: Datchery is not John Jasper, the Princess Puffer, Durdles, Deputy, or even Mayor Sapsea . . . for in our play and in Mr. Dickens' novel, they all appear in scenes with him . . . they are observed to be in his company. And so we are left with the following candidates for the role of Datchery: *(Candidates step forward to form a line)* And may I suggest that we vote the way it is done in amateur theatrical contests? As the handkerchief is held above the head of each candidate, pray applaud for your own favourite in the part of Datchery.

And, do remember, we have larger decisions still to come. Soon we shall be asking you to decide who is the murderer of Edwin Drood. So don't merely vote for whichever cast member is a distant cousin of yours for God's sake. Mr. Throttle, if you please.

(Stage Manager holds handkerchief over appropriate head, identifying candidates)

STAGE MANAGER: Miss Rosa Bud! . . . the Reverend Crisparkle . . . Neville Landless . . . Bazzard . . . and Miss Helena Landless.

(The field is narrowed until the outcome is clearly determined to the satisfaction of all)

CHAIRMAN: Very good. *[Character's name]* is our Datchery tonight! *(To newly-elected Datchery)* You'd best make a quick change of costume. I can see several members of the audience more than ready to assist you in the process. *(New Datchery nods and exits)* And now to a much more—*(He is distracted by a commotion as Nutting, in Victorian street clothes and leading a lap dog on a leash, storms across the stage and up the aisle out of the theatre, never looking back. Chairman may ad lib a parting comment, then continues)* Which brings us, ladies and gentlemen, to a much more serious matter. For now, as in all great mystery stories, we must find ourselves . . . a killer. A culprit. A fiend. In short, the murderer of the dear, departed, vanished, vanquished, late, lamented title character of our play, Edwin Drooood. *(Orchestra members respond vocally a verbal braying. Chairman censures them:)* Oh, shut up. Who killed Edwin Drood . . . Who shall be our Murderer tonight? First for your consideration, ladies and gentlemen, I give you the most obvious candidate for the part: Mr. Clive Paget as John Jasper!

(Paget/Jasper steps forward)

CHAIRMAN: I ask you, is this the face of a murderer? *(He regards Paget/Jasper's matinee smile)* Yes, well. More appropriately, I ask you: could this be all there is to the Mystery of Edwin Drood? That John Jasper, the obvious villain of the piece, did indeed kill his nephew in a hopeless attempt to win the love of the fair Miss Rosa Bud. Ladies and gentlemen: where then the mystery? That's taken the wind out of your sails, Big Mouths, hasn't it, eh? Where then the mystery? Where indeed? So how stand you? For the obvious answer—or for a more perplexing solution? Now certain cast members can be safely eliminated from the bidding: Deputy, Durdles, and my own Sapsea role were, without question, intended for comic relief, and never figure very intimately in the lives of the other characters . . . which leaves us with these remaining characters for the role of Murderer.

(Throttle has handed each suspect a large card bearing their identifying number for the evening. Candidates change position in the "line-up" at each performance. They step forward in turn from left to right and speak their lines)

HELENA: Helena Landless. Did I, in trying to save my brother, bring harm to Edwin Drood? *(Snarls)*

BAZZARD: Bazzard. My need for attention has made me quite mad. Someone stop me before I sing again!

ROSA: Rosa Bud. Why on earth would someone as innocent and pure as myself murder my own true Ned?

NEVILLE LANDLESS: Neville Landless. In all honesty, I cannot recall anything of what transpired once Edwin and I reached the river.

PRINCESS PUFFER: Princess Puffer. Who am I? And what am I?

CRISPARKLE: The Reverend Crisparkle. Have I in some way confused my mission here on earth?

JASPER: John Jasper. I have stood in the cold shade of suspicion since our story began.

CHAIRMAN: Time, ladies and gentlemen, time at last to decide! And may I suggest, for the sake of accuracy, that we vote by a show of hands? Eh? So let's bring up the houselights . . . and we'll begin . . . *(Lights come up and Chairman looks at the assembled audience)* Good lord! Is this what I've been dealing with tonight? Why don't you all join hands and try contacting the living? No matter. Let's proceed post-haste to the voting. Members of our company are even now circulating among you to count your vital votes.

(This is so. As the orchestra plays incidental music, "non-suspect" company members introduce themselves to the various "districts" of the audience and tally their raised-hand votes for "number one, number two", etc. When this is done, they take the results backstage where the votes are totalled. Meanwhile, towards the end of the voting:)

"SETTLING UP THE SCORE" (Voting reprise)

<u>CHAIRMAN AND SUSPECTS</u>:
YOU'VE WATCHED US FROWN, LEER,

PEER AT EVERY SOUL IN THE TOWN,
WE'RE FIT TO FILL THE ROLE . . .

<u>CHAIRMAN</u>:
SETTLE DOWN!
YOUR VERDICT WILL BE CLEAR,
YOUR MURD'RER PICKED IS HERE IN SIGHT!

<u>CHAIRMAN AND SUSPECTS</u>:
TONIGHT YOU CHOSE
FROM CANDIDATES GALORE,
WIN OR LOSE,
YOU'RE GRAND INQUISITOR.
HERE'S THE NEWS:
YOUR JUDGEMENT HAS BEEN PASSED,
YOU'VE SETTLED UP THE SCORE
AT
LAST!

(Throttle crosses to Chairman with a glass of port and whispers in his ear)

CHAIRMAN: Ladies and gentlemen, we have determined the Murderer in our midst! I shall now offer a sip of port to your chosen fiend that he—or she—will know your verdict. And, so that the final dénouement may come as a complete surprise, for the next few moments I strenuously request that you close your eyes, tightly. Pray close your eyes, *now! (He makes no move but continues to speak)* I am offering the port . . . the murderer is drinking it . . . right, you may all open your eyes. *(All suspects wipe their lips)* You see, you cannot trust anyone here tonight! And so, ladies and gentlemen, as our cast departs backstage to learn the result of your decision, I only caution you to prepare for a few unexpected twists and turns, as we serpentine towards the conclusion that you have chosen for us tonight! *(Houselights slowly dim to eerie music)* And so, friends of the Music Hall Royale . . . For the first time . . . and at long last . . . By Your Own Determination . . . The Conclusion . . . the Finale of . . . The Mystery . . .

COMPANY: . . . of Edwin Drooood!

THE CONCLUSION

(Fanfare as the curtain rises on the streets of Cloisterham. It is a bewitching cobalt dawn)

CHAIRMAN: The first chapter of Mr. Dickens' novel was entitled: "The Dawn." Perhaps not coincidentally, the last chapter he wrote was called "The Dawn Again." So, yes, let us begin our last chapter amid the cold grey tendrils of a dim English dawn.

(Puffer is sleeping in a corner of the Cathedral. Rushing by, dressed for travel, is Rosa, bag in hand)

PUFFER: 'Ere, Missy.

(Rosa stops but is still obviously in a hurry)

ROSA: What—what is it?

PUFFER: Can you spare three and six for a Christian soul in distress?

ROSA: We're both Christian souls in distress, I fear, and I have little more than three and six to get me to London.

PUFFER: Running away from something?

ROSA: Yes. At long last, yes. And now I must—

PUFFER: Rosa.

ROSA: How on earth could you know my name?

PUFFER: Know? I've only known you since the day you were born. Only bathed you and fed you . . . *(Puffer slowly gets to her feet)* . . . Don't look at me, Rosa, I don't want you to see me this way. But can you remember your nanny, Rosa, some twelve years ago? Will you look at me now, my own darling girl, and see your Nan instead?

ROSA: Nan . . . somewhere . . . I was six and then she wasn't there any more.

PUFFER: You do remember. God love you, you never really saw your mother, did you? I was the closest thing to that for you. You look exactly like she did before she died.

ROSA: But why did you leave me?

PUFFER: It's a sad story, Rosa, but a common one, I fear.

"THE GARDEN PATH TO HELL" (Puffer)

PUFFER:

I WAS ONCE YOUR NAN,
THEN I MET A MAN—
TALL, AND ALL WITH GOLDEN HAIR,
HE'S WHERE MY END BEGAN.
LET HIM HAVE HIS WAY WITH ME, HE KNEW HIS WAY SO WELL.
LED ME DOWN THE GARDEN PATH TO HELL.

MARRIAGE IN ME 'EAD,
WHAT I GOT INSTEAD
WAS A BED IN CAMDEN TOWN . . . AND THEN TO ME, 'E SAID:
"SHOULD I SEND AROUND A FRIEND, BE NICE TO HIM, THIS SWELL . . .
STROLL HIM DOWN YOUR GARDEN PATH TO HELL."

MAKE YOUR BED OF ROSES, AND SLEEP IN IT,
CUDDLE DEEP IN IT AND PRAY YOU NEVER WAKE.
SOON THE DEADLY POPPIES COME CROPPING UP,
FAIRLY POPPING FROM THE SEEDS OF ONE MISTAKE.

ON MY BACK ALL DAY,
EARNING SATAN'S PAY,
TOOK TO DRINK
SO'S NOT TO THINK
OF WHO'D COME NEXT TO PLAY.
GAVE MY GENT MY EVERY CENT, AND HE GAVE ME FARE-WELL.
LEAVING ME TO WEED THE PATH TO HELL.

LIFE'S A MAZE OF HEDGES THAT PRICKLE YOU,
AS THEY TICKLE YOU, THEY'LL TEAR YOU ALL ABOUT.
STROLLING THROUGH THE MAZE IS AMUSING, TOO,
BUT CONFUSING WHEN YOU FIND THERE'S NO WAY OUT.

LOST MY LOOKS BY THEN,
COULDN'T DRAW THE MEN.
SO I LEARNED A TRADE AND EARNED
MY KEEP WITH DRUGS, AND THEN,
FOUND MYSELF A WICKED SHELF WHERE OPIUM I SELL.
HERE'S A PIPE FOR YOU, SIR,
(PRICE IS FIVE AND TWO, SIR.)
CAN'T YOU SEE THE GARDEN?
IT'S SUCH A LOVELY GARDEN.
I'LL TAKE YOU THERE, I KNOW THE PATH SO WELL
TO HELL. . .
TO HELL.

(Production note: If Rosa has been selected as new Datchery, she exits while song is in progress so as to change into Datchery costume. Puffer is "talking to herself" from thereon)

"PUFFER'S CONFESSION"

PUFFER:

ROSA, MY CHILD, MY OWN,
I'M DEEP ASHAMED YOU WENT THROUGH LIFE ALONE.
AND YET DESPITE MY DRE'FFUL FALL FROM GRACE,
I NEVER ONCE FORGOT YOUR NAME OR FACE.

ONE ICY EVENING, A CLIENT OF MINE
BEGAN TO RAVE AND CRAVE SOME LAUD'NUM WINE,
AND AS HE DRANK A CUP OF SATAN'S BLOOD,
HE MADE THE GREAT MISTAKE OF CRYING "ROSA BUD!"

NOW IT'S ONE THING FOR THEM LIKE ME
TO MIX AND MINGLE WITH THE LIKES OF HE.
WE ARE BOTH MADE FROM GOD'S MOST WRETCHED CLAY
AND MUD . . .
BUT HOW COMES THIS MAN TO CRY OUT "ROSA BUD"!

I CAN'T SEE TOO CLEAR BUT I FOLLOWED HIM HERE.
FINDING OUT WHO WAS WHO, I'VE COME BACK A TIME OR
TWO.
THEN LAST NIGHT, TRACKING ME, WAS THIS MISTER DATCH-
ERY

(Datchery enters)

SO I FOLLOW *HIS* TRACKS TO HIS LODGINGS IN THE BACKS
THO' I HATE TO CONFESS, WELL, I WATCHED THIS MAN
UNDRESS
AND I SAW SUDDENWISE WITHOUT HIS BOLD DISGUISE:

IF DATCHERY IS BAZZARD

AND THE JOB TOOK THEATRICS AND NO FEAR OF HAZARD . . .

DICK DATCHERY IS BAZZARD! *(Go to page 102)*

IF DATCHERY IS REVEREND CRISPARKLE

TOOK A QUICK CHANGE OF ROBES AND A MIND EVEN QUICKER . . .

DICK DATCHERY IS THE VICAR! *(Go to page 104)*

IF DATCHERY IS HELENA LANDLESS

TOOK A BRAVE STRENGTH OF WILL AND MUCH WIT TO HAVE PLANNED THIS . . .

DICK DATCHERY IS MISS LANDLESS! *(Go to page 106)*

IF DATCHERY IS NEVILLE LANDLESS

THO' MY MORALS ARE TILTED, MY EYESIGHT IS LEVEL . . .

DICK DATCHERY IS NEVILLE! *(Go to page 108)*

IF DATCHERY IS ROSA

UNDERNEATH ALL THAT HAIR WAS A FAIR WHITE MIMOSA . . .

DICK DATCHERY IS ROSA! *(Go to page 110)*

"OUT ON A LIMERICK"

IF BAZZARD IS DATCHERY

(Laughing, he pulls off his false beard and wig)

BAZZARD:
YES, IT IS I—I GLADLY REVEAL!
MY JOY IN TELLING ALL I CANNOT CONCEAL.
AUTHOR AM I, AT LEAST OF THIS PAGE.
JOYFULLY, NOW, I TAKE CENTER-STAGE.

MY MOTIVE IN TAKING THIS PART
WAS TO HONE EVEN FURTHER MY ART.
MY THEATRICAL BENT
AND A COSTUME THAT'S LENT
LET ME STRIVE FOR WHAT'S DEAR TO MY HEART:

THE CHANCE FOR SOME PUBLIC ACCLAIM,
JUST A SHRED OF A SECOND OF FAME!
AS A PLAYWRIGHT, A PLOT
TO UNRAVEL SHOULD NOT
POSE A PROBLEM MUCH HARDER TO TAME.

THIS WAS MY GREATEST AUDITION—
TWO DECENT ROLES AT ONE TIME!
FINALLY, SOME RECOGNITION,
STAGING THE SCENE OF THE CRIME,
GOING OUT ON A LIMERICK, OUT ON A LIMERICK,
OUT ON A LIMERICK AIR!

I FOUND A THEATRICAL KIT,
AND AS DATCHERY I DID MY BIT
SO TO CLEAR NEVILLE'S NAME,
(I CONFESS, TO MY SHAME,
'TWAS FOR VANITY, TOO, I ADMIT).
I FOLLOWED JOHN JASPER HIGH-LOW,
FOUND THE DENS HE DESCENDS TO BELOW,
AND WHEN PUFFER CAME HERE
'TWAS IMMEDIATELY CLEAR

MY SUSPICIONS WERE QUITE APROPOS.
SO I CREPT IN THE LODGINGS OF JASPER,
DRESSED IN THIS WIG, WHAT A SIGHT!
THERE I FOUND ROSA BUD'S CLASP, HER
MOTHER'S SHE GAVE DROOD THAT NIGHT.
JASPER TOOK IT FROM NED AFTER HURLING HIM DEAD
TOWARDS THE WEIR RIVERBED, I SUPPOSE.

TELL HIM THAT DATCHERY KNOWS!
AND THE PROOF IS QUITE CLEAR,
LET US BRING JASPER HERE
TO BE TRIED AND THEN TIED UP AND STRUNG!
AND FROM THIS LIMERICK, LET HIM BE HUNG!

(Jasper is hurled from his home by Horace and others towards the audience)

(Go to page 112)

"OUT ON A LIMERICK"

IF CRISPARKLE IS DATCHERY

(Laughing, he pulls off the false beard and wig)

CRISPARKLE:
YES, IT IS I—MY CONSCIENCE IS CLEARED!
I'VE DONNED A FROCK BEFORE BUT NEVER A BEARD.
DEAD NOW IS DATCH'RY, BORN ON A WHIM.
WE CAN DISPENSE WITH LAST RITES FOR HIM.

(Lays down Datchery clothing, blesses it, and removes his own collar defiantly)

THERE ONCE WAS A MAN WHO WAS DRESSED
IN A CLERICAL COLLAR AND VEST,
AND IF ANYONE KNEW
HE HAD FEELINGS LIKE YOU,
THEY'D REPLY TO HIM, "SURELY YOU JEST"!

PARISHIONERS TAKE GREAT OFFENSE
AT ALL PRIESTS WHO WOULD LIKE TO BE GENTS.
WE CAN CONSECRATE WINE,
SPEAK OF "THEE, THOU, OR THINE,"
BUT WE MUSTN'T TAKE HOLD OF EVENTS.

IT WAS A BOLD REVOLUTION,
TURNING MY COLLAR AROUND!
SEEKING THIS PUZZLE'S SOLUTION,
FINDING WHAT WAS TO BE FOUND!
I WAS OUT ON A LIMERICK, OUT ON A LIMERICK,
OUT ON A LIMERICK AIR!

I FOUND A THEATRICAL KIT,
AND AS DATCHERY I DID MY BIT
SO TO CLEAR NEVILLE'S NAME,
(I CONFESS, TO MY SHAME,
'TWAS FOR HELENA, TOO, I ADMIT).
I FOLLOWED JOHN JASPER HIGH-LOW,

FOUND THE DENS HE DESCENDS TO BELOW,
AND WHEN PUFFER CAME HERE
'TWAS IMMEDIATELY CLEAR
MY SUSPICIONS WERE QUITE APROPOS.
SO I CREPT IN THE LODGINGS OF JASPER,
DRESSED IN THIS GARB, WHAT A SIGHT!
THERE I FOUND ROSA BUD'S CLASP, HER
MOTHER'S SHE GAVE DROOD THAT NIGHT.
JASPER TOOK IT FROM NED AFTER HURLING HIM DEAD
TOWARDS THE WEIR RIVERBED, I SUPPOSE.

REVEREND DATCHERY KNOWS!
AND THE PROOF IS QUITE CLEAR,
LET US BRING JASPER HERE
TO BE TRIED AND THEN TIED UP AND STRUNG!
AND FROM THIS LIMERICK, LET HIM BE HUNG!

(Jasper is hurled from his home by Horace and others towards the audience)

(Go to page 112)

"OUT ON A LIMERICK"

IF HELENA IS DATCHERY

(Laughing vibrantly as she pulls the false beard and wig from her face)

HELENA:

THANK GOD FOR THAT! THE SHEEP HAS BEEN SHEARED!
I DON'T KNOW HOW MEN LIVE THROUGH HEAT WITH A BEARD.
GLADLY I SHED THIS TENT OF A COAT.
MY EXPLANATION I NOW EMOTE:

MY MOTIVE IN TAKING THE ROLE
OF A WIGGED AND WHITE-WHISKERED SOUL
WAS TO ABLY DISGUISE
MY MOST FEMININE SIZE
WHEN I'D TAKE AN ENQUIRING STROLL.

FOR STRANGERS WHO'LL CHAT WITH A CHAP,
AND REVEAL THIS AND THAT IN A SNAP,
ARE REMARKABLY LEERY
OF WOMEN WHO QUERY
TOO MUCH. IT'S A GREAT HANDICAP.

SO THIS DISGUISE SAW ME THROUGH IT,
PLAYING THE PART OF A MAN!
REALLY THERE'S NOTHING MUCH TO IT—
MOST ANY ANIMAL CAN!
CLIMBING OUT ON A LIMERICK, OUT ON A LIMERICK,
OUT ON A LIMERICK AIR!

I FOUND A THEATRICAL KIT,
AND AS DATCHERY I DID MY BIT
SO TO CLEAR NEVILLE'S NAME,
(I CONFESS, TO MY SHAME,
'TWAS FOR VENGEANCE AS WELL, I ADMIT).
I FOLLOWED JOHN JASPER HIGH-LOW,
FOUND THE DENS HE DESCENDS TO BELOW,

AND WHEN PUFFER CAME HERE
'TWAS IMMEDIATELY CLEAR
MY SUSPICIONS WERE QUITE APROPOS.
SO I CREPT IN THE LODGINGS OF JASPER,
DRESSED IN THIS GARB, WHAT A SIGHT!
THERE I FOUND ROSA BUD'S CLASP, HER
MOTHER'S SHE GAVE DROOD THAT NIGHT.
JASPER TOOK IT FROM NED AFTER HURLING HIM DEAD
TOWARDS THE WEIR RIVERBED, I SUPPOSE.

"HELENA DATCHERY" KNOWS!
AND THE PROOF IS QUITE CLEAR,
LET US BRING JASPER HERE
TO BE TRIED AND THEN TIED UP AND STRUNG!
AND FROM THIS LIMERICK, LET HIM BE HUNG!

(Jasper is hurled from his home by Horace and others towards the audience)

(Go to page 112)

"OUT ON A LIMERICK"

IF NEVILLE IS DATCHERY

(Laughing, he pulls the wig and beard from his face)

NEVILLE:
THANK GOD FOR THAT—I GLADLY UNMASK!
TO WEAR THIS COAT IN JUNE IS TOO GREAT A TASK.
THERE LIES DICK DATCHERY, BORN ON A WHIM.
WE CAN DISPENSE WITH LAST RITES FOR HIM.

(Takes off coat)

MY MOTIVE IN TAKING THE ROLE
OF A WIGGED AND WHITE-WHISKERED SOUL
WAS TO GET MYSELF BACK
TO THIS CITY AND TRACK
DOWN THE CULPRIT . . . WITH THAT AS MY GOAL,

I HAD ALSO INTENDED TO FIND
JUST WHAT JASPER HAS HAD ON HIS MIND.
MUCH TOO EAGER IS HE
THAT ALL CLOISTERHAM SEE
ME THE MURDERER—GOD, ARE THEY BLIND!

ALL OF THESE PEOPLE SUSPICIOUS
THAT I HAD KILLED EDWIN DROOD,
AND WITH THEIR ANGER SO VICIOUS,
I WORE THIS COSTUME SO CRUDE,
STEPPING OUT ON A LIMERICK, OUT ON A LIMERICK,
OUT ON A LIMERICK AIR!

I FOUND A THEATRICAL KIT,
AND AS DATCHERY I DID MY BIT
SO TO CLEAR MY GOOD NAME
FROM THE BLEMISH OF BLAME,
('TWAS FOR HELENA, TOO, I ADMIT).
I FOLLOWED JOHN JASPER HIGH-LOW,
FOUND THE DENS HE DESCENDS TO BELOW,

AND WHEN PUFFER CAME HERE
'TWAS IMMEDIATELY CLEAR
MY SUSPICIONS WERE QUITE APROPOS.
SO I CREPT IN THE LODGINGS OF JASPER,
DRESSED IN THIS GARB, WHAT A SIGHT!
THERE I FOUND ROSA BUD'S CLASP, HER
MOTHER'S SHE GAVE DROOD THAT NIGHT.
JASPER TOOK IT FROM NED AFTER HURLING HIM DEAD
TOWARDS THE WEIR RIVERBED, I SUPPOSE.

TELL HIM THAT DATCHERY KNOWS!
AND THE PROOF IS QUITE CLEAR,
LET US BRING JASPER HERE
TO BE TRIED AND THEN TIED UP AND STRUNG!
AND FROM THIS LIMERICK, LET HIM BE HUNG!

(Jasper is hurled from his home by Horace and others towards the audience)

(Go to page 112)

"OUT ON A LIMERICK"

IF ROSA IS DATCHERY

(Laughing vibrantly as she pulls the false beard and wig from her face)

<u>ROSA</u>:

THANK GOD FOR THAT! THE SHEEP HAS BEEN SHEARED!
I DON'T KNOW HOW MEN LIVE THROUGH HEAT WITH A BEARD.
GLADLY I SHED THIS TENT OF A COAT.
MY EXPLANATION I NOW EMOTE:

MY MOTIVE IN TAKING THE ROLE
OF A WIGGED AND WHITE-WHISKERED SOUL
WAS TO ABLY DISGUISE
MY MOST FEMININE SIZE
WHEN I'D TAKE AN ENQUIRING STROLL.

FOR STRANGERS WHO'LL CHAT WITH A CHAP,
AND REVEAL THIS AND THAT IN A SNAP,
ARE REMARKABLY LEERY
OF WOMEN WHO QUERY
TOO MUCH. IT'S A GREAT HANDICAP.

SO THIS DISGUISE SAW ME THROUGH IT,
PLAYING THE PART OF A MAN!
REALLY THERE'S NOTHING MUCH TO IT:
MOST ANY ANIMAL CAN!
CLIMBING OUT ON A LIMERICK, OUT ON A LIMERICK,
OUT ON A LIMERICK AIR!

I FOUND A THEATRICAL KIT,
AND AS DATCHERY I DID MY BIT
SO TO CLEAR NEVILLE'S NAME
(I CONFESS, TO MY SHAME,
'TWAS FOR VENGEANCE AS WELL, I ADMIT).
I FOLLOWED JOHN JASPER HIGH-LOW,
FOUND THE DENS HE DESCENDS TO BELOW,

AND AS HE SURFACED HERE
'TWAS IMMEDIATELY CLEAR
MY SUSPICIONS WERE QUITE APROPOS.
SO I CREPT IN THE LODGINGS OF JASPER,
DRESSED IN THIS GARB, WHAT A SIGHT!
THERE I FOUND MY MOTHER'S CLASP, THE
ONE I GAVE EDWIN THAT NIGHT!
JASPER TOOK IT FROM NED AFTER HURLING HIM DEAD
TOWARDS THE WEIR RIVERBED, I SUPPOSE.

"ROSA BUD DATCHERY" KNOWS!
AND THE PROOF IS QUITE CLEAR,
LET US BRING JASPER HERE
TO BE TRIED AND THEN TIED UP AND STRUNG!
AND FROM THIS LIMERICK, LET HIM BE HUNG!

(Jasper is hurled from his home by Horace and others towards the audience)

(Go to page 112)

"JASPER'S CONFESSION"

(Jasper's face goes from the terror of being caught to a maniacal joy)

JASPER:
I WILL NOT LIE
I WISHED NED TO DIE!

(Reflectively)

TWICE DEAD AM I.

A MAN COULD SPLIT IN TWAIN,
YET TO ALL EYES REMAIN
A SOUL GENTEEL WHO CAN CONCEAL
THE VENOM IN HIS BRAIN.
AND IF HE DRAWS UPON THE PAUSE
IN MADNESS OPIUM SMOKE SUPPLIES—
WHY THIS THE GREAT SURPRISE?
THERE ARE TWO MEN IN ME,
AND CUNNING-BRIGHT IS HE
WHO HIDES HIMSELF,
RESIDES HIMSELF
WHERE I'VE NO EYES TO SEE.
BUT NOW I THINK HE'S AT THE BRINK OF BREAKING THROUGH THE DOOR—
I'M IN, HE'S OUT, I'M OUT, HE'S FREE,
I'M FREE, I'M ME ONCE MORE!

(Totally evil now)

HOW MANY TIMES I'VE KILLED THAT DROOD UPON MY FLIGHTS!
MY FLIGHTS THAT BURST THE SMUG PRESUMPTION OF HIS RIGHTS—

HIS RIGHTS AS HEIR, HIS RIGHTS TO SHARE MY ROSA'S BED—
IT TOOK NO SMOKE FOR ME TO PICTURE EDWIN DEAD!
THAT NIGHT I POURED THEM BOTH DEEP CUPS OF LAUDANUM,
AND THEN TO TOAST MY NED AND NEVILLE, I DRANK SOME.
THAT'S WHEN MY GREATEST FLIGHT OF FANCY DID TAKE PLACE:
I WATCHED MY HANDS OUTSTRETCHED TOWARDS EDWIN'S PALE WHITE FACE,
AND IN THE MOONFALL, I SAW MY FINGERS
CLUTCHING HIS NECK SO TIGHTLY,
TOUCHING MY SLEEVE, HE FELL SO LIGHTLY!
MOONFALL THEN FELL ON ME . . .

BUT, GOD, THE DEED WAS MUCH TOO EAS'LY DONE:
AS MUCH AS OVER ONCE IT HAD BEGUN!
SUCH TRAGEDY TO FIN'LLY MAKE THE KILL
AND NOT TO AWAKE TO TASTE THE THRILL.
NOW I'VE CONFESSED!
NOW WE BOTH CAN REST!

(Durdles, who has been loitering about and observing things from a distance, bursts forward bellowing)

DURDLES: No, I can't let it happen! *(To Jasper)* You placed the coat that young Drood wore that night down at the River Weir to throw suspicion on Neville Landless. You're a bad one, Jarsper, when the evil one is inside you! But you're not a murderer! You didn't kill Edwin Drood!

SAPSEA: Durdles . . . let me understand . . . are you saying that John Jasper did not kill his nephew?

DURDLES: Exactly, your lordship, sir. It was a wild night that Christmas Eve, as you'll remember, squire, and I'd sought shelter near Mr. Jarsper's door. That's when I saw One Amongst You throttled Edwin Drood, and in a convenient flash of lightning—I Saw Who It Was!

DURDLES: *(All wait with expectation. Durdles speaks as Cricker)* That was quite a long speech, Bill. Think I could have a quick nip of port?

SAPSEA: Durdles!

DURDLES: Right. Suddenly I see Mr. Jarsper stagger out of his own home under the influence of Potent Medicine. Suddenly he collapses and picks up young Drood, carrying him to the Cathedral and down into the crypt, depositing the body *(He suppresses a laugh)* in your wife's tomb, Mr. Sapsea!

SAPSEA: What?

DURDLES: Yes, I told you there was plenty of room in there—

SAPSEA: But now you must tell us, Durdles: Who Did It?

DURDLES: *(Savouring the moment, he regards the candidates)* Lord love me . . . It was—

(Next line according to audience's vote)

Bazzard! *(Go to page 115)*
Reverend Crisparkle! *(Go to page 117)*
Helena Landless! *(Go to page 119)*
Neville Landless! *(Go to page 121)*
Princess Puffer! *(Go to page 123)*
Rosa Bud! *(Go to page 124)*

IF BAZZARD IS MURDERER:

"BAZZARD'S CONFESSION"

(With his desperate need for one moment in the spotlight, he has become quite mad. His confession is lightly comedic, and his joy in at last being the object of everyone's attention would be almost charmingly touching, were it not for the minor fact that he has murdered Drood to achieve his lifelong ambition. Still, it is hard not to feel happy for him)

BAZZARD:
I SAW THE CHANCE TO BE A LEGEND IN MY TIME,
FOR ALL IN TOWN THOUGHT NEVILLE MIGHT DO VIOLENT CRIME.
TO SOLVE A MYST'RY WOULD PLUCK ME FROM OFF MY SHELF,
SO I ENSURED THE CRIME BY KILLING DROOD MYSELF!

"A MAN COULD GO QUITE MAD" (reprise)

BAZZARD:
DETECTIVES IN COMMAND
MUST HAVE A CASE IN HAND.
TO GAIN ACCLAIM, THEIR SHARE OF FAME,
THE PUBLIC DOES DEMAND
A CONTROVERSIAL CRIME PERVERSE. SHALL
I GO ON TO TELL YOU MORE?
SINCE I HAVE THE FLOOR:

YOUNG NEVILLE HAD BEEN CRUDE,
AND EDWIN DOUBLY RUDE,
SO I SET OUT TO BRING ABOUT
THE DEATH OF EDWIN DROOD!

AND IT TURNED OUT TO BE THIS REGION'S HOTLY-ARGUED RAGE,

AND I KNOW ALL,
I NOW SHOW ALL,
AT LAST I'M CENTER-STAGE!

"NEVER THE LUCK" (reprise)

BAZZARD:
AND I TIED THE KNOT
AROUND HIS NICE NECK
AND HIS HEAD WAS STRUCK NEARBY!
I THOUGHT AS HE FELL
DOWN INTO THE MUCK—
THAT FIN'LLY THE LUCK HAVE I!
THAT FIN'LLY THE LUCK HAVE I!

(After finishing the reprise of "Never the Luck," he accepts the ensuing applause as he were Garrick himself, with slow sweeping gestures and false humility) Thank you, thank you my dear, dear friends. I regret that, in order to attract the attention I've long deserved, I was forced to murder Edwin Drood, but still— *(Shrugging)* I mean, well, there you are. *(Dropping Bazzard and becoming Bax)* And, if I might make so bold, ladies and gentlemen, on behalf of every actor who's ever had to make the most of his three odd lines . . . I say thank you for the chance you've given me this evening and I hope I haven't let you down too bad. Bless you all! *(He resumes his posture as the now completely lunatic Bazzard)*

(Play continues on page 126)

IF CRISPARKLE IS MURDERER:

"CRISPARKLE'S CONFESSION"

(As the following unfolds, we see a gradual change transform the Reverend into a fanatic, easily capable of evil—in God's name)

CRISPARKLE:

IN SAVING SINNERS, THERE'S A CHANCE YOU'LL SIN SOMETIME!

IN SAVING CRIMINALS, ONE MIGHT COMMIT A CRIME!

AND TO PROTECT THE HARMLESS LAMBS WITHIN MY FOLD,

I HAD TO KILL THE WOLF—YOUR CULPRIT YOU BEHOLD!

"A MAN COULD GO QUITE MAD" (reprise)

CRISPARKLE:

SINCE I WAS NEARLY GROWN,

I'VE VERY CLEARLY KNOWN

THAT SATAN WALKS AMONG US WITH NO

FEAR HE SHOULD ATONE.

AND WHEN FAIR ROSA'S MOTHER DIED, THE DEVIL TRIED TO CLAIM 'TWAS ME

KILLED HER IN JEALOUSY!

SO I BECAME A PRIEST

TO BETTER HUNT THE BEAST,

AND WHEN I SAW JOHN JASPER'S PAW

LASH OUT, I KNEW AT LEAST

THAT I'D LOCATED SATAN—HE WAS HATEFUL AND DEPRAVED!

WITH JASPER DEAD, THEN ROSA, NED, AND NEVILLE WOULD BE SAVED!

BUT THE NIGHT WAS FAR FROM BRIGHT,
THICK WITH WET AND THUNDER.
THATCHING FELL DISPATCHED FROM HELL,
SATAN IS A WONDER!
COULD NOT SEE THE ARMS OF ME
STRETCHED OUT WITH SCARF IN HAND.
SAW YOUR COAT AND TIED NED'S THROAT
JUST LIKE A DEADLY WEDDING BAND!

"NO GOOD CAN COME FROM BAD" (reprise)

CRISPARKLE:
SOME YEARS AGO, I THINK I KILLED ANOTHER . . .
ROSA'S MOTHER . . .
NEWLY-WED WAS SHE, THUS DEAD TO ME,
I TOSSED HER OUT TO SEA.
MAY THE LORD BE PRAISED! THOUGH SOME MIGHT CALL ME MAD,
I HAVE RID THE EARTH OF SATAN AND I'M GLAD!
I'M GOOD—FOR GOOD CAN COME FROM BAD!

(Proud of a job well done, he is amiably chirpy) Well, that's that, then! Mind you, it did disarm me for a moment, seeing Jasper alive the morning after I had killed him, but then I realized that once I had slain the devil within him, Satan left Jasper's body, and John was his old Christian self again, eh, John?

JASPER: *(Still stunned by all that has transpired)* You're a sick man, Reverend Crisparkle. You killed my nephew, Edwin Drood. He was wearing my coat and you mistook him for me.

CRISPARKLE: Did I? Did I really? The joke's on me then, isn't it? Oh, and, Rosa, I'm sorry I had to kill your mother. After she married that—man—I detected clear signs of Satan within her and was forced to send her into the cleansing water. You may very well have inherited some of these signs. I should be careful if I were you. Well, I must be off. Bless you all!

(Play continues on page 126)

IF HELENA IS MURDERER:

"HELENA'S CONFESSION"

(Unlike Bazzard, Rosa, and Crisparkle, Helena is not mad. She took the only action she felt would rid her brother and her friend of their tormentor. Her anger now is aimed not only at Jasper but at Cloisterham for placing her in this position)

HELENA:
YOU KNOW THE FURY AND THE FIRE I CAN VENT!
(Whirling on Jasper)
THOUGHT YOU I'D IDLY WAIT WHILE NEVILLE YOU TORMENT?
WITH THIS, HIS ONE, HIS ONLY CHANCE TO START ANEW . . .
YOU SURELY KNOW BY NOW I MEANT TO MURDER *YOU.*

"A MAN COULD GO QUITE MAD" (reprise)

HELENA:
THINK YOU THAT I'M SO BLIND
AS NOT TO READ YOUR MIND
AND WATCH YOU BAIT, MANIPULATE
EACH VICTIM YOU COULD FIND,
AND LET YOU DO TO NEVILLE WHAT YOU'D DONE TO ROSA BUD AS WELL?

I'LL SEE YOU IN HELL!
SOME THING WITHIN ME SNAPPED.
I STARTED TO ADAPT
YOUR GAME OF SIN: TO BLAME MY TWIN,
TO KILL AND NOT BE TRAPPED!
I MADE OF YOU THE VICTIM WHO WOULD MEET HIS END INSTEAD—
MY ONE GREAT FLAW: 'TWAS DROOD I SAW AS YOU!
YOU LIVE! HE'S DEAD!

BUT THE NIGHT WAS FAR FROM BRIGHT,
THICK WITH WET AND THUNDER.
THATCHING FELL DISPATCHED FROM HELL!
IS IT YET A WONDER,
COULD NOT SEE THE ARMS OF ME
STRETCHED OUT WITH SCARF IN HAND.
(To Jasper)
SAW *YOUR* COAT AND TIED NED'S THROAT
JUST LIKE A DEADLY WEDDING BAND!

"NO GOOD CAN COME FROM BAD" (reprise)

HELENA:
I KILLED DROOD!
NOT GLAD TO—I HAD TO!
I SHALL NOT BE COY:
I'M NOT FILLED WITH JOY
THAT I DID DESTROY
ROSA'S DARLING BOY.
IN THESE LATE ADDITIONS, I HAVE NOW REVEALED
CRIMINAL ADMISSIONS HITHERTO CONCEALED.
DAMN YOU ALL, I SWEAR! FULL WARNING YOU HAD HAD!
BAD MUST LEAD TO WORSE—NO GOOD CAN COME FROM BAD,
NO GOOD—NO GOOD CAN COME FROM BAD!!

Odd, isn't it, Crisparkle, that it is I and not the hot-blooded, dark-skinned Neville Landless who brought violence to your smug little English city? I only regret that you're still alive, Jasper. I should have killed you, and would have gladly, but for that coat of yours! Damn the whim that made Edwin wear it—I thought he was you. *(Gently . . . painfully)* And, Rosa, forgive me for taking your lovely boy away from you. Forgive—oh, dear god, Rosa, Reverend Crisparkle, Neville, I need someone's forgiveness. Damn you all! *(Her strong will breaks at last and she weeps)*

(Play continues on page 126)

IF NEVILLE IS MURDERER:

"NEVILLE'S CONFESSION"

(We all assumed the rumors of Neville's violent past were mere whisperings spread by the prejudiced mouths of a small-minded English town . . . and that he was nothing more than a quick-tempered youth, mistreated as a child and misjudged by his peers. Now we are not so sure; perhaps Neville had *to leave Ceylon . . .)*

NEVILLE:
I WAS THE LIKELIEST OF SUSPECTS YOU COULD FIND—
SO QUALIFIED, YOU RULED ME OUT OF SIGHT AND MIND.
OF *COURSE* I KILLED OUR MASTER NED! COULD I FOREGO
THE CHANCE TO GAIN MY PRIDE *AND* ROSA WITH ONE BLOW?

"A MAN COULD GO QUITE MAD" (reprise)

NEVILLE:
A MAN COULD GROW QUITE MAD
FROM BEING JUDGED AS BAD,

AND THIS DESPITE THE QUITE CONTRITE
DEMEANOUR I ONCE HAD.
ONE WISH HAD I: ESTABLISH MY CREDENTIALS AS AN EN-
GLISHMAN!
ONE DOES WHAT ONE CAN.
BUT YOU SAW MY HOT BLOOD,
AND I SAW ROSA BUD.
MY RIVAL, HE, IN RIVALRY,
LET LOOSE A VIOLENT FLOOD.
MORE FOOL WAS I TO EVEN TRY TO KEEP THINGS FROM A
HEAD—
FROM THAT DAY ON ALL HOPE WAS GONE
AND DROOD WAS GOOD AS DEAD!!

BY THE RAGING RIVER BANK,
THUNDERBOLTS TO GUIDE ME,
SOMETHING IN THE WINE WE DRANK
BUILT THE FIRE INSIDE ME.
SO I SHREWDLY LAUGHED WITH DROOD, HE
LEFT, I TRAILED BEHIND.
FOR HIS LAUGHTER DREW ME AFTER HIM WITH MURDER ON
MY MIND!

"NO GOOD CAN COME FROM BAD" (reprise)

NEVILLE:
NO, I COULD NOT BEAR HIS STYLE,
THAT IMPISH, SIMP'RING SMILE HE WORE.
WHILE HE WORE THAT SNEER,
HIS FATE WAS CLEAR.
THE THROATS OF THOSE WHO STRUT
ARE EAS'LY CUT
OR CLOSED. IT'S NOT
THAT TRYING TO GARROTTE.
IN THESE ADDITIONS, I HAVE NOW REVEALED

MURDEROUS ADMISSIONS HITHERTO CONCEALED.
DAMN YOUR LITTLE MINDS! FULL WARNING YOU HAD HAD!
BAD MUST LEAD TO WORSE—NO GOOD CAN COME FROM BAD!
NO GOOD—NO GOOD CAN COME FROM BAD!

(Play continues on page 126)

IF PRINCESS PUFFER IS THE MURDERER:

"PUFFER'S CONFESSION"

(That Puffer tried to kill Jasper does not mark a change in characterization. As she reveals, her only motive was to protect Rosa from the evil side of John Jasper—Puffer's best client—in the only way a woman of the streets and of crime would know. But she has our sympathy, perhaps even our laughter)

PUFFER:
MAY GOD HAVE MERCY, YOUR FORGIVENESS DO I NEED.
MY STRING OF SINS ENDS HERE WITH THIS MOST DREADFUL DEED.
I ONLY MEANT TO SAVE MY ROSA BUD, IT'S TRUE . . .
YOU BASTARD JASPER! CHRIST, I MEANT TO MURDER *YOU!*

(She steps forward, pleading her case directly to us)

"THE WAGES OF SIN" (reprise)

PUFFER:
COULD I SEE MY ROSEBUD THREATENED BY THIS MAN OF MASSIVE SIN?
HE'D REVEALED HIS VILE DESIRES, SO I *HAD* TO DO HIM IN.
TO MY ENDLESS RUINATION, I TOOK SMOKE TO SEE ME THROUGH;

IN MY SWEET HALLUCINATION, I SAW DROOD . . .
(To Jasper)
. . . AND THOUGHT HIM YOU!

SO I SAY TO ALL WHO'LL HEAR ME,
YOU MUST PLAN A MURDER WELL.
YOU MUST VIEW YOUR VICTIM CLEARLY
AS YOU SEND HIM OFF TO HELL.

WHEN I KILLED, 'TWAS WELL-INTENDED!
DRINK AND SMOKE WHAT DID ME IN.
FOR MY CHORES, I'M APPREHENDED!
THEM'S THE WAGES OF SIN!

(Shouts) Everyone now!
(Sings with Company)
THEM'S THE WAGES OF SIN
(Cajoles) Oh bloody 'ell. Don't you know they *hang* women these days? This is undoubtedly my last chorus! C'mon now, everyone!
(Sings with Company)
THEM'S THE WAGES OF SIN!
(Blowing kisses to one and all) Bless you, bless you, and ta-rah!

(Play continues on page 126)

IF ROSA IS MURDERER:

"ROSA BUD'S CONFESSION"

(She laughs hysterically, the laugh of one who is at last able to share a wonderful secret. In her manner and voice there is both Ophelia's madness and an almost sexual sense of release)

ROSA:
WERE YOU SO BLIND YOU COULD NOT SEE I KILLED HIM?
YES!

AND IT WAS WONDERFUL TO DO, I DO CONFESS.
TO HAVE IT DONE, TO DO HIM IN, TO SEE IT THROUGH . . .
(Whirling on Jasper)
YOU SURELY KNOW BY NOW I MEANT TO MURDER *YOU!*

"A MAN COULD GO QUITE MAD" (reprise)

ROSA:
THOUGHT YOU I WAS SO BLIND
AS NOT TO KNOW YOUR MIND,
OF WHAT INTENT EACH COMPLIMENT
YOU CLAIMED YOU MEANT AS KIND?
TO FEEL MYSELF UNROBED AND PROBED WITH EVERY MOVEMENT OF YOUR EYES?

AH, BUT REALIZE:
A CHILD CAN GO QUITE MAD
AND NOT KNOW GOOD FROM BAD
AND CALMLY PLAN
TO KILL A MAN
AND FEEL BUT ONLY GLAD!

TO RID HERSELF—TO BID HERSELF A MURDEROUS GOOD-BYE!
NOT *EDWIN* WHO I SOUGHT, BUT *YOU*—
I MEANT FOR *YOU* TO DIE!

"WHEN SHALL THESE THREE MEET AGAIN?" (reprise)

BUT THE NIGHT WAS FAR FROM BRIGHT,
THICK WITH WET AND THUNDER.
THATCHING FELL DISPATCHED FROM HELL!
IS IT YET A WONDER,
COULD NOT SEE THE ARMS OF ME
STRETCHED OUT WITH SCARF IN HAND.

SAW YOUR COAT *(To Jasper)* AND TIED NED'S THROAT
JUST LIKE A DEADLY WEDDING BAND!

"NO GOOD CAN COME FROM BAD" (reprise)

ROSA:
SO LONG A TIME
THEY'VE THOUGHT THAT I'M
A DRESDEN DOLL, QUITE NAÏVE.
BUT I BELIEVE
THIS PAIN, MY BRAIN MORE TORTURED THAN THEY MIGHT CONCEIVE.
WITH THESE LATE ADDITIONS, I HAVE NOW REVEALED
MURDEROUS ADMISSIONS HITHERTO CONCEALED.

DAMN YOU ALL, I SAY! YOU LET HIM DRIVE ME MAD!
MADNESS LED TO THIS, NO GOOD CAN COME FROM BAD,
NO GOOD—NO GOOD CAN COME FROM BAD!!

(She collapses center-stage, pounding the ground as she weeps hopelessly) I killed my good, true Ned, whom I never stopped loving in the very best of senses . . . I killed him when I meant to kill you, Jasper, you pathetic imitation of manhood! All this because . . . *(Sobs more and her words grow emphatic)* . . . because he was wearing that ludicrous, laughable coat of yours, Jasper! Jasper! Damn your existence and your fraudulent love! Damn Cloisterham that looked the other way when you looked at me in your way! Damn—you—all! *(She collapses, sobbing quietly to herself)*

(IN ALL CASES, NO MATTER WHO THE SELECTED MURDERER IS, THE PLAY NOW CONTINUES. The words "Bless you all" or "Damn you all" are the Chairman's cue to speak up)

CHAIRMAN: Well . . . there is your Murderer! But surely we are also entitled to a Happy Ending? We all have need in our lives for Love . . . Romance . . . or, at this hour of the night, any reasonable facsimile thereof. So it remains for you to resolve one final question: Which two in our story will find that commodity we all seek? Who shall be our lovers tonight? Let us see . . . we are, on the distaff side, left with:

(Chairman omits whoever is no longer on stage)

The lovely MISS ROSA BUD or . . .
The tempestuous HELENA LANDLESS or . . .
The highly experienced PRINCESS PUFFER . . .

Well, which of these ladies would you like to see united in love with one of our remaining male leads? Pray indicate by your applause. *(He names them again and the audience votes by volume of applause)* Fine, right, and then we have a field of well-heeled bachelors available—

DURDLES: Don't forget yourself, Mayor Sapsea!

CHAIRMAN: Yes, very well, and a widower as well. Once again, the kind spattering of your hands as we choose from:

(He omits those not on stage)

MAYOR THOMAS SAPSEA, ESQUIRE
NEVILLE LANDLESS
BAZZARD
THE REVEREND MR. CRISPARKLE
THIS SPECIMEN CALLED DURDLES
JOHN JASPER

(The audience votes, again, by applause)

CHAIRMAN: Right, well, that's your decision and we're stuck with it, I fear. Mr. Purcell, a gentle reprise if you will? It seems we are about to have . . . a love song.

(As Purcell begins his opening introduction, the selected lovers speak their appropriate lines)

(If Rosa is one of the lovers, go to page 129)
(If Helena is one of the lovers, go to page 132)
(If Princess Puffer is one of the lovers, go to page 135)

IF ROSA IS ONE OF THE LOVERS:

ROSA: *(Hopeful, vulnerable)* Reverend . . . Mr. . . . dear Septimus . . . I know you loved my mother—and I believe she made a great error when she married someone other than you. Can you see enough of her in me . . . *(near-seductive)* . . . to take advantage of the fact that you are *not* my father?

CRISPARKLE: What man obtains the chance to regain the lost love of his youth? But, Rosa, I shall love you for what we are and will be, not for what was and might have been!

ROSA: *(Coquettish)* Mr. Bazzard, I should very much like to read your play, *The Thorn of Anxiety.* I sing a little you know . . . perhaps there would be a role in it for me? I need a kinder and more gentle tutor than Mr. Jasper was.

BAZZARD: *(Genuinely)* Miss Rosa . . . since the first day we met . . . the day your Edwin disappeared . . . there has been but one ingenue in the manuscript of my existence!

ROSA: *(Decisively)* Mr. Durdles, after what I've been through, I no longer wish to be a decent and proper English girl! I wish to drink and smoke and let myself become generally dissipated!

DURDLES: *(Lewdly)* Cor, love, if it's degeneracy and ruination you want . . . I'm your man! But, mind you, I've got one bloody hell of a head start!

ROSA: *(Kindly)* Mr. Jasper . . . John . . . you were two men. One of them I saw most often, and feared. The Other had hidden behind his eyes . . . the pain, the anguish of a brilliant, tormented, and gentle soul. As much as I loathed the first Jasper, I was that much drawn to the Other. John . . . which Jasper are you now?

JASPER: Why, we are . . . I mean to say, *I* am the Jasper that loves you singlemost. Come, join me in a song, Rosa, and we shall together be as two . . . I mean as *one!*

ROSA: *(Without hesitation)* Neville, from the moment you first came to Cloisterham, I was drawn to you! It was then I realized that Romantic Love was not something I felt for Ned, but, rather, for you!

NEVILLE: You know that my enmity with Ned was merely because he could not see the treasure he possessed. I vow never to assume your love—but always to earn it!

ROSA: *(Coldly)* Mr. Sapsea, I am no longer interested in being anyone's victim or object of desire. Being an orphan, I hereby will settle for a rich husband who will agree to admire me from a great distance.

SAPSEA: Seize? I shall be most grateful to seize your opportunities posthaste! Ah, Miss Bud, I shall try my best to be the father you wish you never had!

ROSA: Deputy, after being torn asunder by the varied

DEPUTY: Oh, Miss Bud! Oh, dream unexpected!

intentions of John Jasper, Neville Landless, and poor Edwin . . . I should like to begin a new life on Virgin Ground . . . and I think I should like to begin—with you!

(Go to page 138)

Oh, bliss unforeseen! How unprepared I am both for this sudden joy—and for this duet. Help me with the words, won't you, Miss Peregrine?

IF HELENA IS ONE OF THE LOVERS:

HELENA: *(Wryly)* Mr. Bazzard, we both seem to share an interest in amateur theatrics; shall we not meld our mutual talents and leave this limiting city?

BAZZARD: *(Eagerly)* With a life like yours as the source of my inspiration, I think my quill could rise to new heights!

HELENA: *(Truly in love)* Your kindness and goodness has, in its unassuming way, deeply reached my heart, Reverend. Do you think that you could let a warm, strong wind from Ceylon blow away your cold damp memories?

CRISPARKLE: For too long I've committed blasphemy, Helena, by making a Holy Ghost out of Rosa's mother. *You* are life itself, and I wish to join the living!

HELENA: *(Stoically)* Durdles, what you really need in life is someone with a spine of steel to take you in hand and bring out the greatness that lies dormant within you. You shall be a prosperous and renowned stone-mason, and I shall be the Architect of your Future!

DURDLES: *(Lewdly again)* It's a good thing you was raised in India with the elephants, because then living with me won't come as such a surprise!

HELENA: *(Lustily)* Jasper . . . you tried to destroy my brother, my bosom

JASPER: Ah, Helena, if only you could shed your instinctive Eastern shyness!

friend, and your nephew. You are an opium-user, a would-be murderer, a madman, and a musician who ignores all the rules of counterpoint. In short, Mr. Jasper, you are the most fascinatingly attractive man I've met since coming to this silly island and I offer myself to you without a smattering of shame.

Come, my exquisite little dish of chutney, together we shall achieve . . . *Nirvana!*

HELENA: *(In horror)* Neville, the perversity of nature and of this audience tonight has somehow caused me to be incestuously drawn to you. Perhaps you could learn to love me like a brother?

NEVILLE: Helena, I *am* your brother. I suppose we must give this depraved English clique what they desire. You wicked bastards!

HELENA: *(Brisk)* Mr. Sapsea, most Englishmen are mad, useless, boorish, or drunk. You, at least, are not mad. I am willing to marry you on the simple understanding that I will have my own money, life . . . and *bedroom.*

SAPSEA: I suspect you will be a credit both to me and to your race, Miss Landless . . . and I further suspect that "credit" is the appropriate word in this instance!

HELENA: Oh, young Deputy, I seek to enlarge my

DEPUTY: Oh, Miss Landless, I'll be more than

knowledge of this strange land. If you will teach me the secrets of the street life, I will initiate you into the mysteries of the Orient! pleased to drag your fair name into the gutter if you'll elevate my spiritual essence to Nirvana! God bless the British Empire!

(Go to page 138)

IF PUFFER IS ONE OF THE LOVERS:

PUFFER: *(Conspiratorially)* 'Ere, Bazzard, I understand you want to write plays. I've led a life of sin wicked enough to make a score of shameless dramas. 'Ow's about a collaboration? Dip your quill in the ink of my existence, so to speak?

BAZZARD: *(Rakishly)* With a life like yours as the source of my inspiration, I think my quill could rise to new heights!

PUFFER: *(Kittenish)* Father, help a poor sinner who wants to repent. I need the ministrations of a god-fearing man.

CRISPARKLE: Since God has seen fit to deny me the love I so desperately needed . . . then I might as well save a sinner *(Surprisingly rakish)* especially if the sinner is as well versed in her trade as the Princess Puffer!

PUFFER: *(Chummily)* Durdles, we might as well admit it . . . we're destined for each other. I'm the one woman in the whole of England who can't make you feel morally inferior. What say you, love? A quick cuddle before we snuff it?

DURDLES: *(Sweetly)* A squeeze or two from the likes of you, my little Powder-Puff, and I might never touch another drop of drink. That's 'cause *you'd* be pouring it for me! Darlin'!

PUFFER: *(Cold)* You don't fool me, Jasper! You'll be

JASPER: Let us find the answers together and float

all right for a while, and then you'll be needing the pipe again. Who you going to find to make them proper whenever you need them?

on the delirium of *Love!*

PUFFER: *(Knowingly)* 'Ere, love. I understand you're hot-blooded and crave adventure. Stick with me and I'll teach you tricks they don't even know in the Orient!

NEVILLE: Perhaps there's something to be said for England after all!

PUFFER: *(Cunning)* You don't fool me with your pomp and strutting, Sapsea. You used to visit Madame de Lyons' wicked place every fortnight like clockwork, canes and razor-straps was your needs, as I recall. Make me your wife and I won't tell a soul . . . plus, you can get what you used to pay for regular, on the house.

SAPSEA: *(To audience)* What a delightfully cynical finale you've concocted for us this evening. I didn't know you had it in you . . . although, looking around, I suspect that a great number of you have had it in you! *(Gallantly to Puffer/Prysock)* Shall we, Angela?

PUFFER: 'Ere, Deputy, I've got a bargain to strike with you: you give me the passionate energy of your

DEPUTY: Oh, Miss Puffer, I'll be the most willing student you've ever had to discipline! Feel free to

virginal youth and I'll give you the expertise of my chequered past.

drill me for my final exam.

(Go to page 138)

“PERFECT STRANGERS”
(reprise—male and female duet)

SHE:
ONCE WE WERE PERFECT STRANGERS.
HOW STRANGELY MET WERE WE!

HE:
I FIND I NOW ADORE YOU—
OUR BEST HAS YET TO BE.

SHE:
IT SEEMS I’VE LONGED TO HOLD YOU—FATE RULED IT SO!

HE:
YOU LOVE ME, SO THEY’VE TOLD YOU.

SHE:
LET’S NOT RESIST THIS ENDING.

HE:
ONCE WE HAVE KISSED, PRETENDING TAKES NO SKILL,
THIS STRANGENESS MAKES ME THRILL!

SHE AND HE AND ALL:
ONCE WE WERE PERFECT STRANGERS . . .
YET NOW I LOVE YOU PERFECTLY . . . !

CHAIRMAN: But what of Edwin Drood himself? Ah, if only he could speak to us from beyond the grave! What could he tell us . . . what would he say?

(There is an ominous rumbling beneath the ground, aided by a similar rumbling from the orchestra. Suddenly, wonderfully, the crypt of Mrs. Sapsea rises from the earth below, breaking through the floor of the stage as it pushes stone and dusty earth aside. From its doorway emerges a cheery Edwin Drood!)

"THE WRITING ON THE WALL"
(Drood and Company)

DROOD: *(Triumphantly)* I'm alive! Halloo all!

(Cheers from all)

DROOD:
(Spoken introduction)
I AM LAZ'RUS, RISEN FROM THE GRAVE!
QUITE ALIVE YOU FIND ME.
THIS TOMB BEHIND ME
IS WHERE I FACED MY CLOSEST SHAVE.

WHEN I STRUCK MY HEAD AGAINST THE STREET,
I WAS STUNNED, NOT STRICKEN,
(OUR PLOT DOTH THICKEN),
FOR JASPER FLEW ME OFF MY FEET

TO THE CRYPT.
I AWOKE IN DARK BEYOND BELIEF,
AND WHILE ALL ABOVE ME SHOWED THEIR GRIEF,
I WAS SCREAMING FOR MY VERY BREATH,
ONLY MOMENTS FROM DEATH.

YOU HAVE NO IDEA THE SUDDEN STRENGTH
THAT YOU FEEL WITHIN YOU,
THE STEEL AND SINEW,
WHEN FATE STANDS SMILING AT ARM'S-LENGTH.

I ESCAPED FATE! FROM CLOISTERHAM I FLED.
I DID NOT RETURN HERE
'TIL I COULD LEARN HERE
JUST WHO IN HELL WOULD WISH ME DEAD.

(Sung)

BUT MORE THAN THAT,
MORE THAN WHAT SOLUTION FITS THIS CRIME,

WHAT I'VE LEARNED IS THAT LIFE IS BITS OF TIME,
AND YOU FIGHT FOR EVERY TINY SPECK
WHEN YOU'RE HELD BY THE NECK!

I HAVE READ THE WRITING ON THE WALL,
AND THE GREATEST MYST'RY
IS NOT THE HIST'RY
OF JASPER, DROOD, AND ONE AND ALL!

I HAVE MET MY MAKER AND RETURNED!
WHAT ADVICE I'M GIVING
TO ALL THOSE LIVING
IS JUST TO LEARN WHAT I HAVE LEARNED . . .

LIFE IS DEAR.
THERE CAN BE NO VICT'RY IN DEFEAT.
IF OUT-NUMBERED, BEAT A FAST RETREAT
TO THE NEAREST SHELTER AND DIG IN . . .
WHEN YOU LIVE, THEN YOU WIN!

SCRATCH AND CLAW FOR EVERY DAY YOU'RE WORTH!
MAKE THEM DRAG YOU SCREAMING
FROM LIFE, KEEP DREAMING
YOU'LL LIVE FOREVER HERE ON EARTH.

I HAVE READ THE WRITING ON THE WALL,
AND IT'S CLEARLY SPELLED OUT
FOR THOSE WHO'VE HELD OUT
THAT HOLDING ON TO LIFE IS ALL.

IS IT CLEAR?
IF YOU HEAR MY VOICE, THEN YOU'RE ALIVE.
WHAT A BLOODY MARVEL WE SURVIVE
WHEN YOU THINK OF EVERY RISK WE FACE
IN OUR MAD HUMAN RACE!

I HAVE READ THE WRITING ON THE WALL,
TRY TO LIVE FOREVER

AND GIVE UP NEVER
THE FIGHT—YOU'LL NEED THE WHEREWITHAL!
CAN'T YOU READ THE WRITING,
AS I PLEAD,
INCITING YOU TO READ THE WRITING ON THE WALL!

"DON'T QUIT WHILE YOU'RE AHEAD"
(reprise. Chairman and Company)

(The band plays "Don't Quit While You're Ahead" as the company takes their individual and company bows. They acknowledge Mr. Purcell and the band, and join hands to sing)

ALL:
TA-RAH-TA-REE!
BOOM!
BANG IT, BASH IT, OO, GLORY BE!
BOOM!
CLANG IT, CLASH IT, OO-LAH-DEE-DEE!
DON'T QUIT WHILE YOU'RE AHEAD
SING OUT, "THERE'S MORE IN STORE FOR ME"

THE END